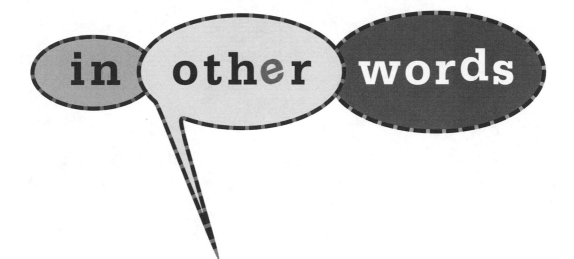

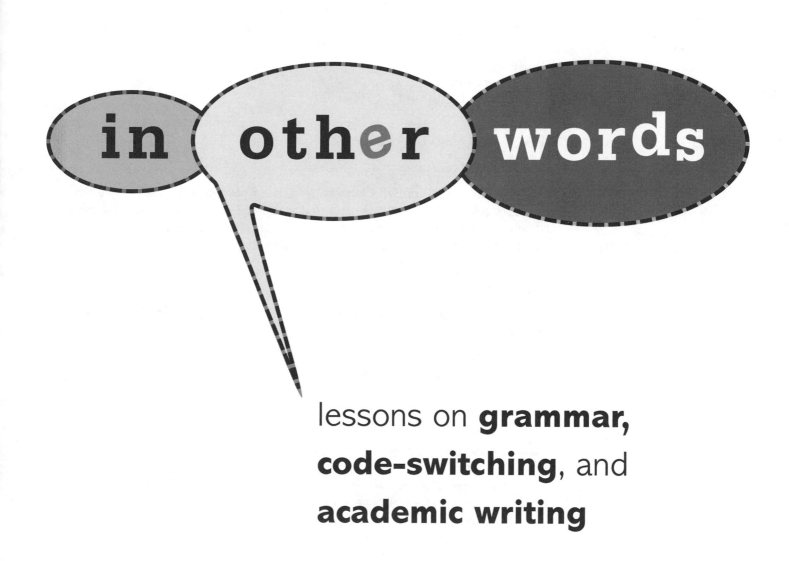

in other words

lessons on **grammar, code-switching**, and **academic writing**

David West Brown

Foreword by Rebecca S. Wheeler

Heinemann, Portsmouth, NH

Heinemann
361 Hanover Street
Portsmouth, NH 03801–3912
www.heinemann.com

Offices and agents throughout the world

The author and publisher wish to thank those who have generously given permission to reprint borrowed material:

Lyrics from "A Noun Is a Person, Place, or Thing" by Lynn Ahrens. Copyright © 1981 by American Broadcasting Music, Inc. Reprinted with permission.

Library of Congress Cataloging-in-Publication Data
Brown, David West.
   In other words : lessons on grammar, code-switching, and academic writing / David West Brown ; foreword by Rebecca S. Wheeler.
       p. c.m.
   Includes bibliographical references.
   ISBN-13: 978-0-325-02188-1
   ISBN-10: 0-325-02188-0
   1. English language—Grammar—Study and teaching (Middle school). 2. English language—Grammar—Study and teaching (Secondary). 3. English language—Composition and exercises—Study and teaching (Middle school). 4. English language—Composition and exercises—Study and teaching (Secondary). 5. Code switching (Linguistics).   I. Title.
   LB1631.B768 2009
   428.2071'2—dc22
                                         2008048278

Editor: Lisa Luedeke
Production editor: Sonja S. Chapman
Cover and interior design: Lisa Fowler
Compositor: Tom Allen, Pear Graphics Design
Manufacturing: Valerie Cooper

Printed in the United States of America on acid-free paper
13 12 11 10 09   ML   1 2 3 4 5

contents

foreword

This book offers readers not simply a gold mine but a treasure trove of English resources. A gold mine, chock-full of priceless veins, nonetheless requires significant work to excavate and fashion the resources into a desired end product. By contrast, a treasure chest offers gems, gold, and riches ready at hand. David West Brown's *In Other Words* offers the reader a treasure trove for the English classroom.

Indeed, Brown's superb classroom resources arrive on the scene just in the nick of time. Already on the twenty-first-century stage, we find scenarios, players, and educational trends on a collision course. We are all aware of the demographic tidal shift within our nation. Study after study reports nationally what we experience locally in our schools: Over the next four decades, the diversity of our student body will increase dramatically as students of color increase from 28 to 50 percent by 2050 (El Nasser 2004).

With diversity of our student population comes diversity of language and culture: School hallways teem and student essays burgeon with cadences and patterns of our students' community, Vernacular English, not to mention the increasing presence of English language learners in our classes. And the cultures to which our students are drawn have more to do with digital mixing, Second Life, and the rhythms of emoticons and instant messaging than with the intricacies of close analysis in reading and clarity or coherence in persuasive writing. And yet, one's ability to write effectively using the lingua franca of Standard English remains a bedrock skill for our global economy.

David West Brown's *In Other Words* provides a beacon for the diverse twenty-first-century English classroom. Brown's goal is clear and unequivocal: He seeks to help students "develop greater facility with Standard English and to help them improve their academic writing" (xi). To this end, Brown, a linguist in English and Education who taught public school for six years (ninth- through twelfth-grade literature), has built a profoundly engaging suite of lessons: These lessons offer "opportunities for students to think about the linguistic choices they make in their daily lives and those they are asked to make in school, to explore English grammar, to recognize some of the characteristics and demands of academic writing, and to develop skills that will help them to more intentionally and successfully negotiate the writing process" (xii).

Brown addresses issues of language and writing that have long perplexed teachers: what to do when students come to school speaking and writing a form of English different from Standard English. Friendly, lively, crystal clear, and accessible, Brown invites the reader on a journey of discovery. With eye-catching examples—language from popular culture, film, TV, and literature—as the subject matter of analysis, he introduces key linguistic concepts (e.g., Vernacular vs. Standard English, dialects, and register) and analytic tools.

As students analyze vernacular and standard uses of *like* ("Like, it's not cool at all" . . . "I'm like 'I'm at my Grandmother's house . . .'") and vernacular uses of *ain't*, students discover the rules underlying their usage, and from there, students induce that all language is patterned and that language varies by setting and by social purpose. Thus, anchoring in the lively and familiar, students develop tools of analytic discernment that will later serve them on their journey to the intricacies of academic writing.

From there, Brown leads students to analyze and discover the systematic patterning of verb tense/aspect and subject-verb agreement across dialects differing across space and time (i.e., "Dat's 'cuz Tony love her too good," in *Their Eyes Were Watching God*; "Yeah, yeah. I done heard everything" [Jaz-Z]; or Shakespeare, "Oh, how this spring of love resembleth/The uncertain glory of an April day"). Students learn the analytic strategy of contrastive analysis and the linguistic choice of code-switching between vernacular and standard grammar as suits the time, place, audience, and communicative purpose.

For the journey, *In Other Words* ensures that both teachers and students have a fully stocked rucksack: Each lesson has two to three pages of background information for teachers, followed by parallel lessons for students (complete with reproducible student activity sheets and teacher answer key). One great feature of this book is the additional teacher resources on nearly every page. Boxes offer teachers "Other Ideas" for organizing lessons or leading discussions, "Important Terms," "Key Points" of the lessons, and "Online Resources" for yet more discovery.

From deft excursions through the terrain of language variation and dialect diversity, Brown leads teachers and students into critical thinking and analysis of the tools and forms of academic writing. From explorations of dictionaries, to topic/comment sentence structure, to the known/new contract, students apply their new analytic skills to discern the intricacies of academic writing and, from there, to produce cohesive academic prose.

Some may well be surprised by Brown's approach to linguistic diversity in the classroom, thinking grammar like "people be lookin' for they little two minutes of fame" (Lil Kim) is just "wrong," that it's "bad English" that has "no place in the classroom." Teachers may worry that to candidly address vernacular language is to "encourage students' habits that will only hurt them in the world." And teachers may at first think that Brown is *teaching* that broken grammar.

Answers to these questions and concerns emerge organically from Brown's work itself. In lesson after lesson, Brown leads the reader to discover the foundational insight of modern linguistics, the key to success in the linguistically diverse classroom: *All language is rule-governed.* The power of this one insight is immense. Once we recognize that when students write or say "I was like, Dude!" or "I be right on top of everything, all the time," they are not making mistakes inside Standard English but instead are following the grammar patterns of the community language variety, we transform the dialectally diverse classroom. We can come to see the students as fully capable and knowledgable about language, perhaps just a variety of English differing from the standard. In turn, this transformation in teachers' perceptions helps invite the students into our educational enterprise.

And so, Brown is not teaching vernacular grammar to students—many of our students are already fluent speakers of their community English variety. Instead, *In Other Words* leads students to develop keen skills of critical thinking and close analysis in familiar terrain—their language of nurture. From that framework for thinking about language, Brown then seamlessly leads students to apply their analytic skills to "other systems with which they are less familiar," such as the academic writing our schools expect. That is, Brown builds upon students' existing knowledge to add new knowledge—of Standard English and the conventions of academic prose.

For ten years, I have worked with teachers on contrastive analysis and code-switching, linguistic insights, and strategies for teaching Standard English in diverse classrooms. And time and time again, K–16 teachers respond, "This approach is so simple, so natural. It's so respectful of our students! Why haven't we ever heard of this before?" It's a good question, for the linguistic cornucopia Brown offers has been well known within the field of linguistics for over half a century. And yet, until recently, linguists have remained largely sequestered in their universities, not venturing out into the applied world of teaching real students in real classrooms. Even more rare is the linguist who has also walked the walk, teaching in the public schools as has David Brown. And more vanishingly rare still is the teacher-linguist who integrates the two fields, giving voice to linguistic insights in a real-world, practical, hands-on, and dynamic way.

David West Brown's *In Other Words* is a tour de force. As a linguist and teacher educator, I am grateful to Brown for bringing his powerhouse of knowledge and real-world savvy to our twenty-first-century English classrooms. Enjoy, as you open the treasure trove before you.

—Rebecca S. Wheeler

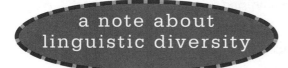

a note about
linguistic diversity

The diversity of the English language can present complex, and sometimes vexing, dilemmas in the composition classroom. How do I respond to students whose English is different from Standard English? Do I correct them? Will correction frustrate or alienate students? Do such concerns matter in light of the pragmatic need to acquire facility with standard norms? In addition to the complexity of such dilemmas, issues related to linguistic diversity and education can provoke strong, passionate responses from teachers, students, parents, and the community.

Such passion is, in part, a product of the relationship between language and identity. Whether one is a Pittsburgher, a Bostonian, a Yooper, or an Angeleno, the way that one speaks can evoke kinship and pride, conveying a sense of where one comes from and who one is. There are also countervailing passions, passions borne from a sense that normative language is an important cultural glue and a practical tool for carrying out the economic, educational, and political work of a society.

The tension between these views of linguistic diversity—one positive, one negative—has been a part of English-speaking culture for a long time. In 1752, for example, Samuel Johnson wrote about cleansing English of its "colloquial barbarisms" and "licentious idioms." Even earlier, ca. 1342, Ranulph Higden lamented the contamination of the English language by contact with Danish and Norman, complaining that "some [people] use strange waffling, chittering, harrying and noisy grease-biting" (Mossé). In contrast, a group that included Thomas Hardy and Edith Wharton composed a manifesto in 1919, arguing that "language is or should be democratic" and that writers should adopt "homespun terms" in order to "preserve the living and popular character of our speech" (Society for Pure English).

The passion that many people have for the English language can present both possibilities and challenges for any teacher wishing to include more language study in the classroom. On the one hand, language can be an engaging subject for students, especially when study includes topics related to their own language use or the language of their friends, communities, or popular culture. Such engagement can be used to build foundational knowledge that then can be extended to the important linguistic work of classrooms. On the other hand, language study that incorporates linguistic features not considered standard, that includes elements of Hardy's and Wharton's "democratic" speech, can be intimidating because many people care so deeply about the English language and, in the long tradition of Johnson and Higden, are skeptical of linguistic diversity and language change. Complicating the picture further are the very strenuous and very real demands on teachers' time—the obligations to meet district, state, and federal targets all while attending to the varied learning and personal needs of the students they encounter every day. Thus, teachers want to get the most bang for the buck, as it were.

In light of these various tensions and complications, I want to be as clear as I can about this book's goals and its orientation to linguistic diversity. First and foremost, the principal goal of the book is to help students develop greater facility with Standard English and to help them improve their academic writing. In trying to achieve that goal, the materials in this book approach students' existing competence with and knowledge of language as a resource to be drawn upon rather than an obstacle to be overcome. If students can become more aware of the linguistic choices they already make, if their inchoate knowledge of English grammar can become more conscious and intentional, their emerging awareness can be applied to the kinds of choices and tasks called for in academic writing.

The materials in this book are designed to both explore and explicate how English works. In doing so, students and teachers may be asked to examine traditional definitions of terms like *grammar* or *correctness*. However, nothing in this book should be taken as an endorsement, tacit or otherwise, of a laissez-faire attitude toward students' work in our classrooms. The work that students produce should always be assessed rigorously. Nor should anything in this book be taken as an endorsement of any particular teaching style or approach to writing. Such decisions, I believe, are best left to teachers with knowledge of their students and schools.

I hope that teachers will take away from this book an enhanced expertise with English grammar, a clearer understanding of specific features of academic writing, and a greater appreciation of students' linguistic competencies, whether those students speak a standard variety of English or not. That new knowledge then can be applied to the teaching of composition and teachers' responses to students' writing.

On this last point—how teachers can use their understanding of diverse grammars to respond to their students' writing—I offer a word of caution. The relationship between a person's spoken language and that same person's writing is complex. The best evidence suggests that novice writers draw on their spoken resources at times as they compose or that they use a hybrid of spoken and written resources as a waypoint to mastery of written Standard English. Thus, if we have diverse speakers of English in our classrooms, we cannot always predict how their spoken language will influence their writing.

Imagine, for example, that the following sentence appears in the essay of a student who does not speak a standard variety of English: "Scout use to be afraid of Boo Radley." How might we explain the phrase *use to*? One possible explanation would be that the student is using an alternative past tense paradigm in her writing—some varieties of English do not mark the past tense with *-ed* as Standard English does. Another possibility would be that the student is using a phonetic spelling—almost all English speakers combine the *d* and the *t* sounds in *used to* if they say the phrase in conversation. Yet another possibility would be that this is a simple miscue. Novice writers (even experienced ones), as we know, do have those in their compositions.

The best that we can do as teachers is to use all our knowledge to uncover patterns in our students' writing. Is this the only instance of an unmarked past tense? Are there other examples of phonetic spellings? An understanding of diverse grammars provides teachers an additional tool for responding to students and their work. Of course, teachers must also respond to far more than word-level or sentence-level features in their students' essays. Simply converting *use to* ➔ *used to* is not necessarily going to make the ideas expressed in that sentence, that paragraph, or that essay any more insightful or eloquent.

For this reason, I would urge potential users of this book not to think of these materials as a method for fixing the myriad challenges facing students who speak varieties of English other than the standard, who are novice writers, or who are both. There are, after all, no panaceas, no quick fixes. Improvement in writing is predicated, in part, on years of reading habits and practice. What these materials offer, instead, are opportunities for students to think about the linguistic choices they make in their daily lives and those they are asked to make in school, to explore English grammar, to recognize some of the characteristics and demands of academic writing, and to develop skills that will help them to more intentionally and successfully negotiate the writing process. These materials are an invitation for teachers and students alike to tackle language as a vital, challenging, and engaging topic of discussion and study.

acknowledgments

I owe a debt of thanks to a great many people for their support, expertise, and generosity in making this book possible. I, first, must recognize Linda Sell and her former twelfth-grade class. They gamely tried out these lessons in their earliest and roughest incarnation. They were unbelievably enthusiastic in their willingness to try out new ideas and always thoughtful in helping to shape what the lessons eventually became. I am also enormously indebted to Dr. Anne Curzan, my advisor and friend, who has guided both the theoretical and practical development of this project at every turn. Likewise, Dr. Mary Schleppegrell contributed greatly in helping me to think through the importance of academic registers as a subject of classroom learning and to compose lessons attending to the study of academic language. Dr. Rebecca Wheeler's input, too, decidedly improved the final shape of the book through both her review and continued support. I would also like to express my gratitude to my former students and colleagues at Sammamish High School, particularly April, Helen, and Kent. Not only have they been incredibly generous with me, but they are doing great things with their talents out in the world. I am tremendously proud to have been your teacher. Thanks, as well, to Lisa Luedeke, my editor, and Kate Montgomery, also at Heinemann, for their encouragement and guidance. Additionally, Dr. John Baugh, Dr. Jeff Reaser, Dr. John Rickford, Dr. Julie Sweetland, and Dr. Walt Wolfram all assisted me in various ways and all produced significant work that precedes and inspired my own. Finally, thanks to all of those who loved, supported, and tolerated me through this writing: my family, especially my parents, and Stephanie and her family, the Batkies.

introduction

OBJECTIVES

- Increase students' facility with Standard English.
- Develop students' academic writing skills.
- Develop students' awareness of how English works.

THIS BOOK FOCUSES SPECIFICALLY ON THE WORKINGS OF THE ENGLISH LANGUAGE AND THE RELATIONSHIP OF LANGUAGE CHOICES TO WRITING. IT IS MADE UP OF THIRTY-FIVE SHORT (APPROXIMATELY FIFTEEN-MINUTE) LESSON PLANS, PROVIDING TEACHERS WITH FLEXIBILITY IN DECIDING WHEN AND HOW FREQUENTLY THE LESSONS ARE IMPLEMENTED IN THEIR CLASSROOM.

Goals of the Book

The goals of this book are to help students

- develop their academic writing skills and
- better understand how the English language works.

Before proceeding to some specifics of the book and background information, I want to acknowledge upfront that writing is hard. Clearly, no one set of teaching materials and strategies can address all the complex, individual challenges writing presents to each of our students. Developing writing skill takes diligence and practice. I hope, however, that the materials and strategies presented here will provide students and teachers alike with practical tools and ways of thinking about language that will clarify some of the demands of academic language and lead to improved student performance.

The lessons in the book center on two basic activities: (1) investigating language and (2) applying new understandings about it. For the first, students and teachers might discuss questions: How is *ain't* used? Who makes dictionaries and how? How is information conveyed in a written sentence? No doubt, some questions may seem unconventional. We are more used to, for example, warning against the use of *ain't* (my grammar checker is cautioning me, even now, with its squiggly red underline) than analyzing how people use it. However, by talking about such questions, I hope that students will begin asking themselves when, why, and how they use certain features of the language: Do I ever use *ain't*? Do I use it with my friends? At school? Have I ever seen it written? Why is it used in these situations? These kinds of questions help students recognize what they already know about language. The purpose of these activities isn't to encourage the use of an informal feature like *ain't* in academic writing. Without exception, students' academic writing should be held to the highest formal standards. Rather, engaging in these questions can help students develop some systematic and explicit knowledge about language. In the case of *ain't*, for

> ### IMPORTANT TERMS
>
> **grammar:** The organization and structure of language that enables people to communicate with each other.
>
> I use *grammatical* to mean that a sentence/utterance/feature adheres to the systematic rules of a language variety for creating comprehensible utterances. A useful distinction here is between *descriptive grammar* and *prescriptive grammar*.

example, students will have to have a grasp of English's tense/aspect system as well as recognize the impact of certain rhetorical choices. This knowledge, then, can be put to use in the second set of activities—application in the practice of academic writing.

Structure of Lessons

Each lesson is designed to be about fifteen minutes long, and the lessons, although interrelated, do not need to be taught in uninterrupted succession. The lessons are designed in this way because they are intended to complement, not displace, the varied and important work that English teachers do. Many English teachers, for example, give their students guidance on composing thesis statements and topic sentences. The lessons presented here on vocabulary, information structure, and conjunctive resources could very well supplement that kind of instruction. This language-focused curriculum, then, is meant to be adaptable to the needs of teachers and their students.

Each lesson is prefaced with a brief summary of background and contextual information. This information should be enough for teachers to implement the lesson successfully without occupying too much of their valuable time. It is quite possible, however, that questions or issues may arise that are not addressed in the information I provide. This isn't necessarily a bad thing. Studying language, like studying any other complex phenomenon, does not always lend itself to straightforward answers. As with a great novel, it is often its ambiguity that proves to be most compelling. Knowing this, however, may not relieve everyone's anxiety. I will try, therefore, to point teachers and students to relevant resources that they can use to investigate further as the need may arise. As teachers and students move through the lessons, I hope that the approaches and strategies presented in the exercises will enable students to puzzle out some of the quandaries of language on their own.

Some Background on Grammar

Before proceeding to the lessons themselves, I want to explain my approach to grammar because it differs somewhat from approaches with which teachers and students might be familiar. Traditionally, grammar is taught as a collection of rules: commas go here, this is a noun, and so on. There is nothing inherently bad about these approaches; there is nothing in them, necessarily, that students must unlearn. Indeed, some of the basic vocabulary of traditional grammar (noun, verb, pronoun, preposition, and so on) is extremely useful for students to know. And knowing where to put your commas? Certainly, that's valuable. Yet, instruction in traditional grammar doesn't seem to have much of an impact on students' writing. Despite this, teachers and students alike have a sense that knowing grammar is important. And, of course, I do too.

It can help to distinguish between two kinds of "grammar" or "grammatical rules": *prescriptive grammar rules* and *descriptive grammar rules.*

Let's look at an example of a grammatical issue we commonly confront as teachers and the potential complications it presents.

Ending a Sentence with a Preposition

There's a commonly understood prescriptive grammar rule regarding prepositions: You can't end a sentence with one. For example, you can't say, "the river that Marlow travels down." Instead, you must say "the river down which Marlow travels." Yet, as speakers of English, we understand the first example perfectly well. And what's more, we say sentences like it all the time without really paying

---

IMPORTANT TERMS

descriptive grammar: Rules of language that describe how people communicate.

Descriptive grammer rules are generally associated with the spoken language, and generally speaking, linguists record these rules. Examples of descriptive rules for Standard English include: adjectives precede the nouns they modify; regular nouns form the plural by adding -s; indefinite pronouns such as *everyone* are often referred back to with plural pronouns because they are semantically plural (e.g., "Everyone should mind their manners"). Descriptive rules for African American English (which differ from Standard English) include: two or more negative forms can be used to express negation; invariant *be* expresses habitual action (for example, "He always be bothering me"). So when linguists ask if a sentence is grammatical, they are really asking whether or not it adheres to the systematic patterns of a particular language variety.

When I use the term *grammatical*, I am using it in a descriptive sense. This is not meant to imply that it isn't important for students to master the prescriptive grammatical rules—as we all know, they will be judged on their control of them in many formal situations. But it is helpful to make a distinction between the two, so that Standard English is not seen as objectively "more right" than other varieties of English and so that students understand that there are two kinds of "rules."

much attention. That's because English is a Germanic language and as such is capable of producing perfectly logical and understandable sentences that end with a preposition. The rule that one shouldn't is, in fact, a relic of the eighteenth century. At that time, many scholars believed that English was too unsophisticated to communicate the profound ideas of the day. The language most suitable for that task was Latin. It was thought that English could be polished by making it look more like Latin and, therefore, be made more substantial. In Latin, a grammatical sentence cannot end in a preposition. To do so would be the equivalent of something like, "the river that Marlow down travels." It wouldn't make any sense. That Latin rule, then, was applied to English in order to improve the language and has been with us ever since. And similar rules have stuck around: that you can't split an infinitive (in Latin an infinitive is one word, in English two), or that you can't use multiple negation (an application of mathematical logic to language).

Because some of these rules are artificial applications of one language to another, they can sometimes cause problems when you try to use them uniformly. Let's look at the rule governing sentences with final prepositions again. In English, prepositions are extraordinarily useful words. We normally think of them as indicating spatial relationships (*above, below, beside,* and so on). Prepositions, however, can do many other things. One common function of prepositions is to act as part of a verb. For example, *down* is often attached to *weigh,* making the verb *to weigh down,* as in "the foreboding that weighs Marlow down." Used in this way, *down* carries some of its prepositional meaning (it conveys a sense of downwardness), but is really part of the verb. Therefore, it would seem strange to say, "the foreboding down which Marlow weighs."

The rule governing sentences with final prepositions, then, isn't really a *grammatical* rule at all in the descriptive sense. In other words, it doesn't describe how English syntax works. It is, instead, a convention of usage, which doesn't mean that the convention is worthless. It is, perhaps, useful to think of these conventions like table manners. Manners don't describe how people eat food; they tell people how they should eat in light of certain social expectations.

IMPORTANT TERMS

dialect: A variety of a language that is systematically distinct from other varieties.

Appalachian English is distinct from Standard English, which is distinct from African American English. Each dialect has its own particular vocabulary, pronunciations, verb and pronoun systems, and so on. Yet, each is a variety of English and, to a greater or lesser degree, is intelligible to speakers of other dialects. As a term, *dialect* is most often used to refer to spoken language but can refer to written language as well.

Not ending a sentence with a preposition might be akin to not eating with your fingers. Violation of the etiquette might be penalized in some social situations and unnoticed or even encouraged in others. It is useful to know the convention, but it is also important to know when, why, and how to break to it.

Key Points
- -
- Facility with Standard English is an important tool for educational success.
- Languages vary over time, region, and use.
- All dialect varieties are systematic and logical.
- Standard English can be learned as an addition to rather than a replacement for alternative varieties of English.
- Learning grammar is important and doesn't have to be boring.

Some Background on Dialect and Register

All living languages, like English, vary over time (language change), over geographic region and social groups (dialects), and over different types of use (register and genre).

The difference between usage conventions and grammar points to the way that grammar, as a concept, is conceived of and presented in this book. Grammar is far more than a well-defined, ageless set of prescriptive rules. It is a complex intersection of linguistic systems and social expectations that is sometimes ambiguous and always changing. One way to think about this complexity is through changes over time. Consider how different the language of Shakespeare or Chaucer or *Beowulf* is from ours. And language change doesn't just occur over centuries. It occurs during our lifetimes. Younger people, for example, are far more inclined to use *like* than older people. Some may think of the newer uses of *like* as sloppy or quasi-literate, but there is actually a system to its use, a grammar.

In addition to changing over time, English, at any given time, varies community by community. Such variations are commonly referred to as *dialects*, and each dialect has its own specific grammar. For example, later in the book, I have a lesson on reflexive pronouns—contrasting the system in Standard English from the system used in African American English and some other dialects. Fill in the blank at the end of the sentence with a reflexive pronoun: I did it ___. You would end the sentence with *myself*. Now change the pronoun to the second person. You would end the sentence with *yourself*. Now change the pronoun to the third person masculine. If you speak a standard variety, you would end the sentence with *himself*. Note the change in the pattern: *myself* and *yourself* are possessive, and *himself* is objective. This doesn't happen in all English dialects. In some, the pattern holds: *myself, yourself, hisself*. Why does Standard

IMPORTANT TERMS

register: A collection of linguistic features customarily used for a particular rhetorical practice.

A register is something like what is popularly referred to as -*speak*: business-speak, political-speak, jock-speak, and so on. Underlying these terms is a recognition that there is a particular way of communicating associated with a particular purpose. Register describes the vocabulary, sentence structures, verb types, and other features that are common to practices like business communication or academic writing.

genre: A group of texts with common characteristics.

There are all sorts of academic genres: the lab report, the mathematical proof, the history essay, the short-answer exam, and so on. As English teachers, we are well attuned to genres and teach genre features all the time—thesis statements, topic sentences, particular paragraph structures— without necessarily thinking of them as describing the literary analysis genre. But there are also other features of the literary analysis genre that we may be less aware of—like the use of densely packed noun phrases in topic sentences—that may be useful for our students to work on.

English break the pattern but others maintain it? Although the answer is unclear, the different pronoun systems serve as a small example of the ways in which the grammars of different dialects can vary.

In addition to varying by dialect, the English language also varies by use. If increased Standard English facility is the broad goal for our students, think about the vast array of written uses to which Standard English is put: newspaper articles, business reports, government records, technical reports, advertising copy, instruction manuals, school essays, and so on. For each of these uses, there has evolved sets of characteristic features: vocabularies, sentence types, organizational structures. These features are often called *registers* (we can talk about academic registers, for example) and the types of texts that are frequently reproduced are called *genres* (the literary essay being an important genre for us). The expected features of registers and genres are what people often associate with good writing in a given field. However, even very skilled writers and readers are not always explicitly aware of the features that they frequently use and respond to. For example, I am prone to use the comment "needs development" in the margins of my students' essays. If a student asks about the comment, I can tell him or her that they need to take an idea and explain it further. But what does that actually look like? How do I explain the characteristics of a well-developed sentence? Or how sentences should connect one to another to create a cohesive and well-developed passage? These questions present altogether different challenges.

ONLINE RESOURCES

Origins of Some Prescriptive Grammar Rules

www.uoregon.edu/~spike/ling290/badEnglish.html

Language Variation and Change—What Is Ebonics?

www.lsadc.org/info/ling-fields-change.cfm

Do You Speak American?

www.pbs.org/speak/education

At this point, all of the challenges—those presented by the variations in both dialects and registers—may seem overwhelming. How can we, as teachers, possibly know the complex grammars of the dialects that our students speak as well as the grammars of all of the registers they will need to know? Although the task before us is certainly not a simple one, the good news is that we do not need to know all of these things. Teaching grammar is a funny subject because, unlike math, say, any high school student who is a native speaker of the language already has internalized all of the grammatical rules for whatever variety of English he or she speaks. This book is trying to get them to develop an understanding of that grammatical system, a framework for thinking about language, and then extend and apply that understanding to other systems with which they are less familiar. I am trying to find a way to approach grammar that will help students to develop the facility and confidence to make choices as they compose and revise their writing. As I said before, this is no easy task, but one that I think is both important and achievable.

An Example of Register Variation

Consider the three following excerpts about surfing.

1. It is unclear why surfing has found a broader respectability. Some point to the initial public offering of Quiksilver, the board apparel and accessories company, in 1986 as a catalyst. Perhaps reflecting surfing's laid-back roots, concrete figures on participation are hard to come by. Two million people consider themselves active surfers in the United States, twice as many as 20 years ago, according to Action Sports Retailer, the leading board-sports industry trade show.

2. Modern surfboards are constructed of a plastic foam core that is shaped by hand or machine and then covered with a shell of fiberglass and resin. Individual surfboards can vary in dimensions. The high performance surfboards used by top professional competitors are typically about 1.8 to 2 m (6 to 6.5 ft) long, 47 cm (18.5 in) wide, less than 6 cm (2.5 in) thick, and weigh about 2.7 kg (6 lb). These boards are also known as shortboards. On the other end of the surfboard spectrum is the longboard. Most longboards are 2.7 m (9 ft) long, 51 to 56 cm (20 to 22 in) wide, and about the same thickness as shortboards. They weigh less than 7 kg (15 lb).

3. Wow . . . definitely a night and day scenario. Headed out to DH early yesterday morning for a quick surf on the Bing. Small kine waves rolling through with hardly a wisp of wind. Super fun to be loggin it again. Good chance for me to get back into shape before going back to the northshore. Managed to get one killer wave . . . it walled up about waist high for a nice long hang ten, then back stepped as it pitched a bit to get a teeny weeny coverup, more like water splashing on my shoulder, but felt good. Zipped through that section and the wave opened up again for a another noseride with a fade back. Good fun and all to myself!

All three texts are written in Standard English, but all are written in distinctly different registers. Using our intuitions about language, we could probably guess their contexts. The first is from a *New York Times* article (Higgins 2007) on the growing popularity and gentrification of surfing. We might notice the speculative language (*unclear*, *Perhaps*). We might also notice the attributions to authorities (*Some*, *Action Sports Retailer*) and the preponderance of numbers (*1986*, *concrete figures*, *Two million*, *20 years ago*), all of which are characteristic of newspaper writing. The second excerpt is from a Microsoft Encarta Online Encyclopedia article on surfing. Why might we suspect this is from an informational source like an encyclopedia? We might, for example, notice the repetitive and related sentence beginnings, which is a hallmark of some informational texts (*Modern surfboards*, *Individual surfboards*, *The high performance surfboards*, *These boards*, *Most longboards*, *They*). The third excerpt is from a surfer's blog, Bagus Surf (Williams 2007). In this case, we might notice the frequent appearance of the first person (even where it is implied), or the use of specific vocabulary items like *kine*, *hang ten*, *coverup*, *noseride*, and so on. There are, of course, many other observations we might make, but the basic idea is one that is fairly straightforward: These texts are recognizable and describable according to their rhetorical purposes.

Using the Lessons

Each lesson is approximately ten to twenty minutes long. By keeping them relatively short, I've tried to make them adaptable to teachers' full schedules. Teachers can implement them once a week, twice a week, or in whatever arrangement that works for them and their students.

I've also made a commitment to using real-world examples in the lessons. Many examples are drawn from literature and others are from popular culture and actual student writing. I hope that the literary examples will help teachers integrate these lessons into their existing content, and I hope that the other references will help make the lessons less abstract and more relevant for the students.

Another feature you will likely notice is the inclusion of technical vocabulary like *preposition*, *predicative adjective*, and so on. Knowing such terms isn't necessary for either students or teachers to complete the lessons. However, I do not feel that these terms are something to avoid. People learn technical vocabulary by engaging and wrestling with it. I've tried to provide definitions where useful. And for teachers with an interest in pursuing these terms and concepts in greater detail, the places where the terms arise are potential opportunities for further study.

Finally, I've included whenever possible all of the material necessary to complete the lessons. The materials have been drawn from my collections, research, and experience. There is, however, no substitute for teachers' knowledge of their own students, schools, and communities. These lessons represent an introduction and an invitation to working with language and grammar. By no means do they represent the only way to engage this material or all of the language instruction that students need. I hope and encourage teachers to take what I've presented here and create lessons that work for their own classrooms.

Terminology and Variation in English

Some of the exercises in this book use the terms *Vernacular* and *Standard* to describe varieties of English or grammatical features of those varieties like verb and pronoun paradigms. By working through the curriculum, students and teachers will shape definitions of these terms for themselves. However, I would like to offer at least some background—a framework around which users of the book can build their understandings.

On the surface, Standard English may seem like a fairly intuitive concept. Many students conceptualize Standard English as "proper" language. Others may think of it as the language of mainstream culture, the language of the school and the workplace, or the language of wider communication. It is the variety of English most often used in formal writing, whether academic or professional, and is one variety among many. Varieties of English (or specific linguistic features, like *a-* prefixing in the Appalachian English verb system: *a-hunting we will go* . . .) that are distinct from Standard English are here referred to as *Vernacular*. Vernacular varieties are, generally, more frequently spoken than written; though, as we will see, Vernacular features are used in writing of all kinds.

In making the distinction between Standard and Vernacular, it is, first, important to recognize that this book examines differences in grammar and syntax but not differences in pronunciation or phonology (say, whether *pin* and *pen* sound the same or different).[1] Second, we need to differentiate the grammatical features that distinguish a variety (descriptive grammar) from usage conventions (prescriptive grammar), as I noted earlier. In exploring both Standard and Vernacular varieties of English, this book focuses on *descriptive* contrasts. Though, as I also noted, prescriptive grammar is important, and descriptive knowledge can help students better understand prescriptive conventions.

Finally, for the sake of clarity these materials refer to "Standard English" as if it were an unambiguous and consistent entity. However, no language variety is entirely uniform. That is, two speakers of the same variety of English may not use exactly the same features. For example, *y'all*, as a second person plural pronoun, is a feature of Southern American English, and there is a high probability that a speaker of Southern American English will use that feature. However, a speaker of Southern American English may use a different pronoun—maybe *all y'all*, maybe *you*—and that difference does not mean that the speaker is any more or less a user of that variety.

.

Thus, we might think of language variation as determined by groups of features and probabilities that exist along a continuum rather than in separate, distinct boxes. In addition, variation happens not just across communities (Vernacular vs. Standard), but also across other dimensions. These materials, for instance, explore registers (Informal vs. Formal), or how language varies according to use.

To illustrate the multidimensionality of variation, let's consider a feature that is examined in the book: *be* + *like* as used to report speech or the so-called quotative *like* (*I was like, "Dude!"*). In terms of Vernacular versus Standard, most people would probably consider this a Vernacular feature; it certainly contrasts with the written standard, where we would expect other verbs such as *say* or *state*. As a spoken feature, however, the distinction is somewhat less clear because quotative *like* is used by speakers of many varieties including speakers who predominantly use Standard features. On a Vernacular/Standard scale, then, we might place quotative *like* somewhere near the middle on the Vernacular side of the scale. On an informal/formal scale, however, we might place quotative *like* more definitively on the informal side of the scale.

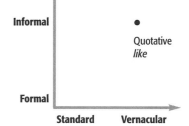

Variation by community and use, of course, are just two of the many dimensions we could plot. English varies by time—we could compare features of Shakespeare's English to contemporary English or even some features used by students to those used by teachers. It varies by mode—we could compare features of conversational English to written English. There are, in fact, any number of variations that we could consider.

The multidimensional variation of English is a principal insight that, I hope, teachers and students can take away from this book. With that insight, teachers and students can apply the practices that they use to compare/contrast Vernacular and Standard dialects or formal and informal registers to other kinds of variation. As a tool for extending the linguistic concepts presented in the book, the simple T-graph that is used in many of the contrastive exercises can function as a core graphic organizer.[2] Teachers can have students collect examples of any feature (feature X) from students' own writing, classroom reading, or other sources to fill the left column. Then, based on the parameters the teacher has established, students can fill in corresponding contrastive features (feature Y) in the right column.

Take the example of Shakespearean versus contemporary language. We might have students create a contrastive chart for X = Shakespearean verbs in *Hamlet* and Y = modern verbs.

Shakespearean verbs in Hamlet	Modern verbs
1. Alexander returneth into dust; the dust is earth . . .	returns
2. Thou art a scholar; speak to it, Horatio.	are
3. Would, like the spring that turneth wood to stone . . .	turns

Students could create similar contrastive charts for conversational versus academic vocabulary, dependent versus independent clauses, hypotactic versus paratactic sentences, or any other contrastive pair of features that we might want our students to be aware of and attentive to. Exploring variation in this way makes the materials in this book relevant to students regardless of the particular variety of English they speak. I hope these materials prompt students to think about not just one variety of English or another, but more fundamentally about how English works.

Talking to Students About Linguistic Diversity

At the beginning of the book, I observed that exploring linguistic diversity in the classroom can sometimes be challenging because of the competing passions the subject can arouse. On this score, students are no different than any other population. Additionally, students are accustomed to the rhythms and conventions of the classroom. So if a teacher were to put *ain't* on the board and ask students to discuss how it works without any prefacing context or discussion, we would expect a great deal of puzzlement if not outright resistance. Students would certainly ask, "Why are we doing this?"

I would, therefore, encourage anyone inclined to use these materials to be prepared, from the very first lesson, to articulate their reasons for pursuing this line of study in his or her classroom. Certainly, teachers are welcome to adopt some of the objectives that I have set forth.

- Students will consider the linguistic choices they make in their daily lives and those they are asked to make in school.
- They will explore English grammar.
- They will recognize some of the characteristics and demands of academic writing.
- And they will develop skills that will help them to more intentionally and successfully negotiate the writing process.

Better yet, teachers will be clear in their own minds about their reasons for using this book and will be ready and willing to explain those reasons to their students. Additionally, for those teachers with the inclination and the time (which I know is a fraught issue), I think it can be productive to give a hearing to any concerns students might have.

Another potential issue is that a student might say something like, "I never use *ain't*, so why should I learn about it?" In order to respond to such a concern, I would direct teachers to the preceding discussion about terminology and variation. In summary, these lessons are not aimed simply at teaching students about *ain't*, habitual *be,* or any other discrete grammatical feature. Part of what students can learn from these materials is an approach to language, a habit of mind. They can develop strategies that allow them puzzle out the workings of language for themselves. An analogy would be learning to plot the flight of a baseball in physics. Students would not solve such a problem because they play baseball. The solution to the problem, rather, illustrates the interaction among mass, velocity, and gravity—underlying laws of physics that can be applied to a host of other problems. So too, by understanding how a particular linguistic feature functions, a student can induce more generalized rules about the systems of English.

Discovering Some Grammatical Rules for <u>Like</u>

Key Points

- *Like* has Standard as well as other uses.
- Even though some consider Vernacular uses of *like* to be indiscriminant, such uses are rule-governed and grammatical.
- As a Vernacular feature, *like* can be used as a quotative and a discourse marker.

Background for Teachers

Why am I starting by having students investigate *like*? Given that my stated goal is to extend students' facility with Standard English, this might seem an odd point of departure. Early in the unit, I want to get students thinking and talking about language. Part of that process is developing a vocabulary and a framework

> "In order to figure out how like *is being used, we need to ask ourselves a couple questions: How is* like *functioning, and is there a pattern?"*

Important Terms

discourse marker: A word or phrase that divides or organizes spoken discourse into units.

English has many discourse markers, for example *I mean, you know, well,* and *okay.* As a discourse marker, *like* can serve several functions. It can be a placeholder, in that case working similarly to *uh* or *um.* It can intensify or focus the listener on certain information. Sometimes this kind of usage comes before hyperbole: "Fine I just got a, a lot of reading to do, like five hundred years of it, so . . ." (The *OC,* "The Heights"). Conversely, *like* can function as a hedge when the speaker is unsure of the information that follows: "She looks a little older don't you think, like, maybe she's in college" (*The OC,* "The Rager").

for understanding how the language they use every day works. *Like* is a word that makes for interesting and productive opening lessons for several reasons.

- Most speakers of English are familiar with the use of *like*.
- *Like* has various uses, and its use is quite complex (and rule-governed).
- Students will begin contrasting one system that employs *like* with one that does not, thereby setting some groundwork for more extensive contrastive analysis.
- Though some consider it uneducated or illiterate, *like* remains in productive use.
- The continued use of *like* invites questions as to its social and rhetorical effects.

Like has been a part of the English language since at least the tenth century, and probably well before, and has all sorts of accepted uses in Standard English: as a verb and a preposition, among others. In the late '70s or early '80s, some new uses began to be popularized and through movies like *Valley Girl* and *Clueless* have become associated with the speech of Southern Californian adolescent girls, although the use is much more extensive. These uses are considered by many people to be the careless (and sometimes irritating) speech of young people, yet the use of *like*, if anything, is continuing to spread. What's more, the stereotypical uses of *like* in "valley girl" speech have rules. Consider the boldfaced *likes* in the following quotations (I'll talk about the underlined one shortly).

> **Like**, it's not cool at all! **Like**, it's all this stuff that tastes <u>like</u> nothing and it's supposed to be so good for you. Why couldn't they, **like**, open a Pizza Hut or something? (*Valley Girl*)

> This weekend he called me up and he's all "Where were you today?" and I'm **like** "I'm at my Grandmother's house . . ." (*Clueless*)

In order to figure out how *like* is being used, we need to ask ourselves a couple questions: How is *like* functioning, and is there a pattern? In the first example, *like* is being used to emphasize words and phrases, to focus the listener's attention on certain parts of the narrative. It's being used, in technical terms, as a *discourse marker*. In the second example, *like* is being used with *to be* as a verb to introduce quoted speech. This type of verb is called a *quotative*. (Note that *be + all* ["he's all . . ."] earlier in the example serves the same function.) One interesting characteristic of quotative *like* is that it doesn't necessarily introduce what someone actually said. Often, it precedes parodied speech or what someone supposedly thought or felt.

The purpose of these first exercises isn't for students to memorize the technical terms for particular grammatical functions. The purpose here is to get them thinking about language, how it functions, and what structural patterns they can puzzle out. Finding patterns isn't always easy, and the function of a particular word can sometimes be ambiguous, especially with a word such as

IMPORTANT TERMS

preposition: A word that expresses the relationship of a noun or noun equivalent to another noun, adjective, or verb; typically relationships of location, duration, direction, and manner. Some common prepositions are *of, in, to, for, on, with, at, by,* and *from.*

conjunction: The most common conjunctions are coordinating conjunctions, which connect words to words, phrases to phrases, or clauses to clauses. Some frequently used examples are *and, but, or,* and *so.* The second most common conjunctions are subordinating conjunctions, which connect a dependent clause to a main clause. Some frequently used examples are *because, when, after,* and *if.*

Like can be both a preposition and a conjunction. If *like* is used as a preposition, what follows it will be a noun or noun equivalent. If *like* is used as a conjunction, it is a subordinating conjunction, which means what follows will be an entire clause. In this quotation from *The Beautiful and Damned,* by Fitzgerald, *like* is a preposition: "He was a short man with a mustache resting <u>like</u> **a small white cloud beneath his undistinguished nose.**" What follows <u>like</u> is the equivalent of a noun; you could substitute it for what is bolded. In the next quotation from *Huckleberry Finn,* by Twain, *like* is a conjunction: "She took up the spinning stick, and it looked <u>like</u> **it was all she could do to keep from giving him a crack with it.**" What follows *like* is a clause; there is a subject and verb. What is bolded could stand alone as a sentence.

like that can serve many different purposes. Consider the third *like* in the first example, which is underlined. Is it functioning as a preposition comparing the taste of "all this stuff" to nothing? Or as a discourse marker intensifying the nothingness of the taste? I would argue that it's a preposition because it controls the noun that follows and because a discourse marker can be taken out of a phrase and that phrase will still make sense. In this case, if you take out *like* you're left with "that tastes nothing," which doesn't work. A student, however, might make the case for a discourse marker. That's okay. At this point, we don't expect them to have the expertise to make that kind of distinction. In such cases, the goal is for students to be able to make a reasoned case for their position and to work through any ambiguities as best they can. It is important for them to begin to be more aware of language and the way it works.

ONLINE RESOURCES

Like, Quote Me

www.pbs.org/speak/words/
sezwho/like/

Like It or Not, a Discourse Marker Making Its Mark on a Wider Stage

www.voanews.com/
specialenglish/archive/
2006-05/2006-05-09-voa5.cfm

The Way Teens Talk, Like, Serves a Purpose

www.jsonline.com/story/
index.aspx?id=71334

Discourse Marker Like and So

https://secure.ldc.upenn.edu/
intranet/Annotation/MDE/
guidelines/2003/like1.html

lesson plan **1**   Introduction

MATERIALS

None

OTHER IDEAS

Another way to organize the discussion in Procedure 2 would be to ask small groups or individual students to generate a list of, say, three ways that distinguishes their language at school, at home, and with their friends.

Most often it is speech that influences writing, but sometimes writing influences speech. Can students think of any instances that they've heard speech that they thought sounded more like writing? What was their reaction?

Objectives

• Students will begin to consider the fact that they make language choices all the time when they speak and write.

Procedures

1. Begin by giving a quick version of the objectives for the book: that we will spend some time this semester looking at how language works and use what we learn to improve our writing.

2. Ask students, "How is the way you talk at home or with your friends different from the language you use in your schoolwork?" They might respond by saying at home or with friends they're more relaxed, but at school they're more formal. Discuss their responses. If they characterize school language as more formal or more proper, ask what they mean by that. How would they describe *formality*?

3. Students may respond to the previous discussion by saying they use more slang with their friends. If they do, ask them for examples of the slang they use outside of school (keeping it appropriate, of course). If slang does not come up, ask them if they can think of examples of words they use with friends but not at school. I, for example, having grown up in California, have the residual habit of using *dude*, a word that doesn't frequently make it into my school compositions. Write their list on the board or on an overhead.

4. You might conclude by observing that we all make choices when we speak or write. Many times those choices are not conscious or seem natural (i.e., "Of course, I don't talk with my friends the way I talk to my teacher! They'd think I was a loser!"). But sometimes, the way we speak influences the way we write, without our realizing it. We'll be talking about some of those possible influences.

lesson plan 2 Uses of Like

Objectives

- Students will work with a variety of uses for *like*.
- Students will begin to recognize one of the systematic differences between Standard English and other varieties.

Procedures

1. We are now going to get into some more technical material about language and parts of speech. Begin by asking students what is the stereotypical way that teenagers use *like*. Ask them for examples. What do they think of when they hear someone use *like* in these ways? Then ask students if they would consider these uses to be Standard or not and why.

2. Write the following sentences on the board or have them prepared on an overhead.
   A. We're gonna be living in real cities with like real, nonbotoxed, nonplastic people. (*The OC*, "The Game")
   B. Yeah, I mean, if you don't like it anymore. (*Bring It On*)
   C. I wanna get outta here and then . . . soon as it's time I'm all like, "No, no I'm not ready." (*The OC*, "The Pot Stirrer")
   D. She's like a Martian. (*Mean Girls*)

3. Before evaluating the sentences, you will need to introduce the term *Vernacular*. You don't need to take a lot of time with this. You might tell them that, in very general terms, *Vernacular* describes varieties of English that are different from Standard English and that the more they work with the term, the clearer it will become. A definition is also provided on the student handout.

4. For each of the four sentences, ask them if they would consider the use of *like* to be Standard or Vernacular and why. You might remind them to only evaluate the use of *like*, not any of the other features of the sentence.

5. Distribute copies of Handout 2:1.

6. Review the directions with students. Then have students complete the handout either individually or in small groups.

7. Review their answers. Responses may vary, so have students explain and defend their choices.

MATERIALS

1. Copies of Handout 2:1
2. Overhead with sample sentences (optional)

OTHER IDEAS

Discussing Standard uses of *like* is a natural place to reinforce the definition of a simile and how it is different from a metaphor.

ANSWER KEY

Procedure 2

A. Vernacular
B. Standard
C. Vernacular
D. Standard or Vernacular, is the speaker using it to emphasize *Martian* or to make a simile?

Handout 2:1

1. V
2. S
3. V
4. V
5. V
6. S
7. V
8. V
9. S
10. V

Handout 2:1 **Uses of <u>Like</u>**

For each quotation, decide if the use of *like* that is underlined is Standard (S) or Vernacular (V), and write your answer in the space provided. One way of thinking about the difference would be to determine if the particular use of *like* would be more likely to be found in school, for example on an essay, or out of school, maybe in a casual conversation among teenagers. **But be careful.** You are only judging the use of *like*. Although the rest of the quotation may have slang or other informal features, the use of *like* may, in fact, be Standard.

_____ 1. If I would blow her off to hang out with Kyle, she'd be <u>like</u>, "Why didn't you call me back?" And I'd be <u>like</u>, "Why are you so obsessed with me?" (*Mean Girls*)

_____ 2. It's <u>like</u> I have ESPN or something. (*Mean Girls*)

_____ 3. Yeah, I know. I've been, <u>like</u>, totally busy with school and practice and stuff. (*Bring It On*)

_____ 4. She, <u>like</u>, writes all over her notebook, "Mrs. Aaron Samuels." (*Mean Girls*)

_____ 5. First you were <u>like</u>, "Whoa!" And then we were all <u>like</u>, "Whoa!" And then you were <u>like</u>, "Whoa." (*Finding Nemo*)

_____ 6. No. He cannot blow you off <u>like</u> that. (*Mean Girls*)

_____ 7. And Janis was, <u>like</u>, weirdly jealous of him. (*Mean Girls*)

_____ 8. Zach, I love girls and I love comics, the two *do not* mix okay. It's gonna be <u>like</u>, "Let's make their outfits cuter." (*The OC*, "The Rager")

_____ 9. People totally <u>like</u> Brutus just as much as they <u>like</u> Caesar. (*Mean Girls*)

_____ 10. Sailing is <u>like</u> so not the fastest way to get anywhere. I mean if you would have flown you would've gotten there a lot sooner. (*The OC*, "The Heights")

IMPORTANT TERMS

vernacular: A variety of English that has systematic grammatical differences from Standard English.

For example, Appalachian English uses a- prefixing in some verbs (a-hunting we will go . . .), and Standard English does not. But just because the use of a– before some verbs is different, does not mean that it is random. There are rules. Can you guess which one of these follows the rules?

A. But Tom Sawyer, he a-hunted me up.

B. I was a-studying over my text.

C. The a-whooping went on.

Answer: B. The sentence is from *The Adventures of Huckleberry Finn.*

lesson plan 3   How <u>Like</u> Functions

Objectives

* Students will begin identifying word functions, which will help them learn parts of speech.

Procedures

1. Begin by telling students that they will figure out rules that describe how people use *like*. If you want to give them an analogy, ask students to think of something that they do that has rules and imagine trying to figure out the rules of that activity without knowing anything about it or having anyone explain it to them. For example, I'm a bit of a sports junkie. But what if I knew nothing about football, needed to know the rules, and had only a stack of game tapes to help me? How would I go about figuring out the rules that determine how the game is played?

2. Distribute copies of Handout 3:1.

3. Review the directions with students. You might do some guided practice by completing the first function as a class. You could begin with quotation A. What other quotations use *like* in the same way as quotation A? The answer would be quotations E and H. So students would write, "A, E, and H" under function 1. Then you can ask students to describe that function. They might respond that it comes before a quotation or that it can substitute for *say*. Any such description would be fine.

4. Have students complete the handout as a class, in small groups, or individually.

5. Review their responses. There is almost certainly going to be some variation, which is fine. Moments of disagreement can make for fruitful discussions. Where students disagree, ask them to explain and defend their responses.

MATERIALS

Copies of Handout 3:1

OTHER IDEAS

Students may well put B and F together under the same function. This isn't bad, but can they distinguish the two? One way is to do a substitution test. What words can substitute for *like* in B? One answer would be *as if*. Can *as if* substitute for *like* in I? It can't. *Like* in B is a conjunction and *like* in I is a preposition. *Like* as a conjunction is actually considered by some to be too informal for academic writing. What is preferred? *As if*. Knowing the substitution rule can be handy.

ANSWER KEY

Handout 3:1

Answers will vary, but here is an example of a possible response.

Function 1: A, E, H
Description: It comes before something someone supposedly said or thought.

Function 2: B
Description: It can be substituted for *as if*.

Function 3: C, D, G, J
Description: It adds emphasis to what comes after *like*.

Function 4: F
Description: It makes a comparison.

Function 5: I
Description: It's an action.

Handout 3:1 **How <u>Like</u> Functions**

In the previous exercise you were asked to decide if the following examples of *like* were Standard or not. In this exercise, you are going to figure out how *like* works.

Take the following quotations and group them according to how *like* functions. In other words, which uses of *like* do you think are similar? Write the letter of those uses that you think are similar in the same box. For example, consider the first sentence. Do you see any other sentences that you think use *like* in the same way as it is used in that first sentence? Write the letters of those sentences in the box under function 1. Note that we have provided space for five different functions, **but you do not have to use all five of the functions or you may create more if you need them.**

When you have finished grouping the sentences, write a description of each function for *like*. A description simply answers the question, "Why have you grouped those particular sentences together?" If you are having difficulty writing an explanation, another approach is to think of a word or words that could be substituted for *like*.

A. If I would blow her off to hang out with Kyle, she'd be <u>like</u>, "Why didn't you call me back?" And I'd be <u>like</u>, "Why are you so obsessed with me?" (*Mean Girls*)

B. It's <u>like</u> I have ESPN or something. (*Mean Girls*)

C. Yeah, I know. I've been, <u>like</u>, totally busy with school and practice and stuff. (*Bring It On*)

D. She, <u>like</u>, writes all over her notebook, "Mrs. Aaron Samuels." (*Mean Girls*)

E. First you were <u>like</u>, "Whoa!" And then we were all <u>like</u>, "Whoa!" And then you were <u>like</u>, "Whoa." (*Finding Nemo*)

F. No. He cannot blow you off <u>like</u> that. (*Mean Girls*)

G. And Janis was, <u>like</u>, weirdly jealous of him. (*Mean Girls*)

H. Zach, I love girls and I love comics, the two *do not* mix okay. It's gonna be <u>like</u>, "Let's make their outfits cuter." (*The OC*, "The Rager")

I. People totally <u>like</u> Brutus just as much as they <u>like</u> Caesar. (*Mean Girls*)

J. Sailing is <u>like</u> so not the fastest way to get anywhere. I mean if you would have flown you would've gotten there a lot sooner. (*The OC*, "The Heights")

Function 1	Function 2	Function 3	Function 4	Function 5
Quotations (by letter):	Quotations (by letter):	Quotations (by letter):	Quotations (by letter):	Quotations (by letter):
Description:	Description:	Description:	Description:	Description:

lesson plan 4   Quotatives and Discourse Markers

Objectives

- Students will review what they have learned about *like*.
- Students will begin to formalize some of their knowledge about parts of speech.

Procedures

1. You might start by telling students that they will review what they have learned about *like*.
2. Distribute copies of Handout 4:1.
3. Have students read the handout individually or read it aloud as a class.
4. Have students respond to the questions at the bottom of the handout.
   - Which of the sentences uses *like* as a quotative?
   - Which of the sentences uses *like* as a discourse marker?
   - You may also ask the two bonus questions: Which of the sentences uses *like* as a verb? As a preposition?

OTHER IDEAS

If students had an easy time with Lesson 3, this review may be too redundant. An alternative would be to have students come up with or bring in their own examples of *like*. Students could then answer the questions at the bottom of the handout based on their examples.

You can ask students for other examples of quotatives not generally considered Standard (*is all* and *goes,* for example). Likewise, you can ask them to generate a list of Standard quotatives.

This is also a good place to explore the difference between direct and indirect speech. Some say that *like* can only be used for direct speech. (In writing, the convention is to put direct speech in quotations: *She said, "I'm scared."*) Others contend that it can be used for indirect speech as well. (Indirect speech is reported and doesn't require quotations: *She said that she was scared.* Note, too, the differences in pronouns.) You can have students go out and gather samples of quotative *like* by listening to people around them speak and writing down what they hear. Can they find any examples of indirect use of *like*?

MATERIALS

1. Copies of Handout 4:1
2. Copies of the ten sentences from Handout 2:1 or 3:1 either on an overhead or on the board

ANSWER KEY

Handout 4:1
  Quotative: 4
  Discourse Marker: 1
  Verb: 2
  Preposition: 3

Handout 4:1 Quotatives and Discourse Markers

BACKGROUND FOR STUDENTS

Like has been a part of the English language since at least the tenth century, and probably well before, and has all sorts of accepted uses in Standard English: as a verb, a preposition, and a conjunction (though its use as a conjunction is disputed), among others. In the late '70s or early '80s, some new uses began to be popularized, and through movies like *Valley Girl* and *Clueless* have become associated with the speech of Southern Californian adolescent girls. These uses are considered by many people to be the careless (and sometimes irritating) speech of young people, yet the use of *like*, if anything, is continuing to spread. What's more, the stereotypical uses of *like* in "valley girl" speech have rules. Consider the following quotations.

> **Like**, it's not cool at all! **Like**, it's all this stuff that tastes <u>like</u> nothing and it's supposed to be so good for you. Why couldn't they, **like**, open a Pizza Hut or something? (*Valley Girl*)

> This weekend he called me up and he's all "Where were you today?" and I'm **like** "I'm at my Grandmother's house . . ." (*Clueless*)

In order to figure out how *like* is being used, we need to ask ourselves a couple of questions: How is *like* functioning, and is there a pattern? In the first example, *like* is being used to emphasize certain words and phrases, to focus the listener's attention on certain parts of the narrative. It's being used, in technical terms, as a *discourse marker*. In the second example, *like* is being used with *to be* as a verb to introduce quoted or parodied speech, thoughts, or feelings. This type of verb is called a *quotative*.

What about the third *like* in the first example, the one that's underlined? Is it a discourse marker? One test for a discourse marker is that it can be removed and the sentence will still make sense. So we could take out *like* from the first sentence and we would have "It's not cool at all!" It still makes sense. Now, can you take out the *like* that's underlined? Doesn't work. So how is it functioning? Do you know what part of speech it is?

With your teacher, answer the following questions based on the following quotations from *The OC*.

1. We do have, *like*, five hundred TV screens all to ourselves. ("The Mallpisode")

2. It's a little something I *like* to call the truth. ("The Mallpisode")

3. It's *like* Goonies meets Die Hard by way of Mission Impossible . . . with I think a slight hint of National Treasure thrown in. ("The Mallpisode")

4. You were *like*, "I have a laundry list of things to do." ("The Rager")

Which of the preceding examples of *like* is a quotative? Which is a discourse marker?

Bonus questions: Which is a verb? Which is a preposition?

KEY POINTS

- *Like* has both Standard and Vernacular uses.
- Even though some consider Vernacular uses of *like* to be indiscriminant, such uses are rule-governed and grammatical.
- As a Standard feature, *like* can be used as a verb, preposition, or conjunction (maybe).
- As a Vernacular feature, *like* can be used as a quotative and a discourse marker.

IMPORTANT TERMS

discourse marker: A word or phrase that divides spoken discourse into units.

English has many discourse markers, for example *I mean*, *you know*, *well,* and *okay*. As a discourse marker, *like* can serve several functions. It can be a placeholder, in that case working similarly to *uh* or *um*. It can intensify or focus the listener on certain information. Sometimes this kind of usage comes before hyperbole: "Fine I just got a, a lot of reading to do, **like** five hundred years of it, so . . ." (*The OC*, "The Heights"). Conversely, *like* can function as a hedge when the speaker is unsure of the information that follows: "She looks a little older don't you think, **like**, maybe she's in college" (*The OC*, "The Rager").

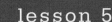

Discovering Some Grammatical Rules for Ain't

> *"It's not suprising that ain't survives. What is, perhaps, surprising is the variety of persons and tenses for which ain't can be used."*

Key Points

- *Ain't* has been in the English language for centuries and is still used by many speakers.
- *Ain't* can substitute for the negative of *am, is,* and *are* as they are used in the present, present progressive, and future (when the future is formed by *to be going to*).
- *Ain't* can substitute for the negative of *has* and *have* as they are used in the present perfect and as auxiliary verbs with got.
- Ain't can substitute for contractions of *do not, does not,* and *did not.*

Background for Teachers

In the next lesson, we will do a short exercise with *ain't* that mirrors what we just did with *like.* The purpose is to reinforce the idea of the systematicity of language and to further tap students' intuitions about language.

In the late seventeenth century, *ain't* started out as *an't*, a contracted form of *am not* and *are not.* Because contracted negative forms of *to be* exist for all persons and tenses (*isn't, aren't, wasn't, weren't*) but Standard English doesn't have

---

IMPORTANT TERMS

tense: A change in the form of a verb indicating when an action or state takes place in time. (For regular verbs in Standard English this change is the addition of an *-ed* ending, for example, to indicate past time.)

Note: Technically verb tense locates an action in time and verb aspect indicates the perception of an action by a speaker (like whether that action is complete or habitual). What is commonly called the progressive tense, therefore, is really a progressive aspect.

one for the present tense first-person singular (*I am not*), perhaps it's not surprising that *ain't* survives for that purpose. After all, what is more logical about saying "aren't I?" than "ain't I?"

What is, perhaps, surprising is the variety of persons and tenses for which *ain't* can be used. Below is a partial list with examples from some literary and other sources.

Though not all speakers use all these different forms of *ain't*, we can make some generalizations: (1) it can substitute for the negative of *am*, *is*, and *are* as they are used in the present, present progressive, and future (when the future is formed by *to be going to*), (2) it can substitute for the negative of *has* and *have* as they are used in the present perfect and as auxiliary verbs with *got*, and (3) it can substitute for *didn't*.

And a note: It isn't necessary for students to memorize the technical names of the verb tense/aspect system (though you may certainly introduce some terms if you wish). I would, however, urge some caution. Contrasting tense/aspect systems across varieties is not always straightforward. Consider the following excerpts from *The Color Purple* (Walker 1992).

1. My mama dead. She **die** screaming and cussing. She **scream** at me. She **cuss** at me.
2. . . . you **could have knock** me over with a feather.
3. I think she thought she **love** him.

What would you identify as the contrasting features in Standard English for the verbs in bold? In excerpts 1 and 3, the contrast is in how the past tense is marked for regular verbs: *die* versus *died*, *scream* versus *screamed*, *cuss* versus *cussed*, and *love* versus *loved*. In this particular Vernacular, the past is unmarked for regular verbs, and in Standard English the past is marked with + *-ed*.

However, in excerpt 2, the contrast is not about tense at all. Tense describes a change in the form (spelling or pronunciation) of a verb or the addition of an ending. English has only two tenses, present and past. The contrast in excerpt 2 is simply the main verb (*knock*) and whether or not it is marked with an *-ed* ending (*knock* vs. *knocked*).

Important Terms

progressive aspect: An aspect indicating an ongoing or continuing action. In Standard English, the progressive combines a form of *be* with a main verb (V + *-ing*, or what's commonly called the present participle).[3]

perfect aspect: An aspect indicating the relationship between a previous state or action and one occurring at a later time or describing a previous state or action from the point of view of a later time. In Standard English, the perfect aspect can be expressed in the past, present, and future, as well as progressively and conditionally. In the past, present, and future, the perfect aspect combines the appropriate form of *have* with a main verb (V + *-ed/en*, or what's commonly called the past participle).

Some Examples of Ain't

Contraction of *to be* in the present tense:

> *First-person singular (am not):* I **ain't** much good, but I could cook and tend the chickens and hoe the garden some. (*Of Mice and Men,* Steinbeck)

> *First-person plural (are not):* We **ain't** burglars. That ain't no sort of style. We are highwaymen. (*The Adventures of Huckleberry Finn,* Twain)

> *Third-person singular (is not):* There **ain't** one thing in this world I can do about folks except laugh, so I'm gonna join the circus and laugh my head off. (*To Kill a Mockingbird,* Lee)

> *Third-person plural (are not):* Even then, they **ain't** worth the bullet it takes to shoot 'em. (*To Kill a Mockingbird,* Lee)

> *Second-person singular (are not):* Humph! Y'all let her worry yuh. You **ain't** like me. (*Their Eyes Were Watching God,* Hurston)

Contraction of *to be* in the progressive aspect:

> *Progressive (is not):* You never oughta drink water when it **ain't** running, Lennie. (*Of Mice and Men,* Steinbeck)

> *Progressive, indicating future (are not):* I'll give him the work tickets, but you **ain't** gonna say a word. (*Of Mice and Men,* Steinbeck)

Contraction of *to have* in the perfect aspect:

> *Present perfect (has not):* Scout yonder's been readin' ever since she was born, and she **ain't** even started to school yet. (*To Kill a Mockingbird,* Lee)

> *or*

> Ah **ain't** had a thing on mah stomach today exceptin' mah hand. (*Their Eyes Were Watching God,* Hurston)

> *Perfect progressive (have not):* Ah **ain't** been sleepin' so good for more'n uh week . . . (*Their Eyes Were Watching God,* Hurston)

Contraction of *to have* in *to have got:*

> *Negative of "to have got":* Well, we **ain't** got no ketchup. (*Of Mice and Men,* Steinbeck)

> *or*

> We **ain't** got to stay here. (*Of Mice and Men,* Steinbeck)

Contraction of *to do* in the past tense:

> *Past tense (did not):* What tow-head? I **hain't** see no tow-head. (*The Adventures of Huckleberry Finn,* Twain)

ONLINE RESOURCES

Tense and Time
www.phon.ucl.ac.uk/home/ dick/tta/tense/tense.htm

Verb Tense Chart
http://owl.english.purdue.ed u/handouts/esl/esltensverb .html

lesson plan **5** Uses of <u>Ain't</u>

MATERIALS

An overhead or copies of Handout 5:1

OTHER IDEAS

Can students identify the verbs in the original sentences? (1. *like to run*, *ain't*; 2. *ain't want to do*, *sang*, *pulled*; 3. *ain't had*; 4. *have spoken*, *ain't*, *discounting*, *making*; 5. *goes*, *ain't gonna change*, *ain't gonna change*, *hang* (*around*), *become*) Is *not* part of the verb? This can also be a good place to review the verb *to be*.

ANSWER KEY

Handout 5:1

1. isn't
2. don't
3. haven't
4. aren't
5. am not

Question: *Ain't* can substitute for *to be*, *to do*, and *to have*.

Objectives

- Students will be able to recognize verbs.
- Students will be able to substitute Standard uses of *to be, to have,* and *to do* for Vernacular uses of *ain't.*

Procedures

1. Begin by telling students that they will figure out rules that describe how people use *ain't* in the same way that they figured out the rules for *like.*

2. Distribute Handout 5:1.

3. Review the directions. You might do the first sentence as a class.

4. Then, have students complete the other four individually or in small groups.

5. Review their answers as a class. Students may need a reminder about what the infinitive of a verb is, and they may have to be prompted about the verb *to be.*

Handout 5:1 **Uses of <u>Ain't</u>**

For each quotation, you will decide what *ain't* stands for in Standard English. Take, for example, the phrase "It ain't over till it's over." *Isn't* could be substituted for *ain't*. Be careful. The answer ain't always obvious.

1. Least like to run against? He ain't in the race. (George Herbert Walker Bush in a Larry King interview)
   What could be substituted for *ain't*? _____

2. There's a lot of things in my life that I ain't really want to do no more. (Gary Sheffield in ABC News Interview)
   What could be substituted for *ain't*? _____

3. We ain't really had a whole lot of laps out there because of the weather. (Dale Earnhardt, Jr. in NASCAR interview)
   What could be substituted for *ain't*? _____

4. The people have spoken and they ain't happy about my recent column discounting the Rockets' chances of making the playoffs without Yao Ming. (Mannix, *Sports Illustrated*)
   What could be substituted for *ain't*? _____

5. As far as the VMAs were concerned, Kanye received the upper hand. I ain't going to front. (50 Cent in *Billboard* interview by Crosley)
   What could be substituted for *ain't*? _____

Based on the above examples, *ain't* can substitute for what three verbs (use the infinitive form)?

IMPORTANT TERMS

infinitive: The form of a verb that is not marked for person, number, or time. Often, the infinitive is expressed with the particle *to*: *to write, to dance, to dis, to email, to be,* and so on.

The Social Uses of <u>Ain't</u>

> "Given that ain't *is so* often socially stigmatized and has been for such a long time, why do people still use it?"

Key Points

- *Ain't* communicates social as well as grammatical information.
- The social significance of words changes over time.
- Even though *ain't* is frequently stigmatized, it is still regularly used in mainstream publications.
- The changing social significance of words like *ain't* is often reflected in how they are labeled and defined in dictionaries.

Background for Teachers

Now that we've done some work on how *ain't* is used, we want to discuss with students why it is used, and why, for example, *ain't* is considered so much worse than, say, *don't* or *can't*. In 1781, Reverend John Witherspoon condemned a whole list of "vulgar abbreviations," including "an't, can't, han't, don't, should'nt, would'nt, could'nt, &c." Of course, most of these contractions are no longer considered "vulgar," except for *ain't*. Many scholars have pointed out that one reason *ain't* may have been so criticized is that its form does not clearly correspond to the forms for which it is a contraction (*am, is, are, has, have,* and in some dialects, *does* and *do*); however, one could make a similar point about the contraction *won't*. Although *ain't* has been condemned in prescriptive resources and many speakers believe the word is somehow fundamentally corrupt (which accounts for the uproar after the publication of Webster's Third in 1961, which recognized the word's widespread use without a derogatory label), as we saw in the previous lessons, there is nothing grammatically "wrong" with *ain't*. Be that as it may, given that *ain't* is so often socially stigmatized and has been for such a long time, why do people still use it?

For some speakers, *ain't* is simply a systematic part of their dialect—in particular, a part of their system for marking negation in various verb tenses and aspects—and its use operates, most of the time, below the level of consciousness. For other speakers, it can be a stylistic choice—a linguistic feature they can use if they want to sound or appear in a particular way. And for all listeners, *ain't* carries a great deal of social information. In this next lesson, students will examine some of those social meanings. Some of the students' perceptions may echo those of Witherspoon and later grammar watchdogs, and most, if not all, will at least be aware of those perceptions, even if they don't share them. Other perceptions may be quite different. Students may perceive the use of *ain't* in some situations as more cool or real than the alternatives.

Even in writing, which adheres more to Standard English norms than speech, the use of *ain't* crops up, often tapping into these latter perceptions of *ain't* as authentic. Recently, the *New York Times* ran the headline, "For the Mets, Two Out of Three Ain't Bad" (Shpigel), and another newspaper declared "Diplomacy Ain't What It Used to Be" (Kamen). On the World Wide Web where writers frequently play with grammatical convention, one popular site goes by the name of "Ain't It Cool." As evidence of the tension between competing perceptions of *ain't*, another website offers up the following definition: "Bad Grammerian—people who think the word 'ain't' is cool" (my English teacher instincts just can't ignore the ironic spelling of *grammerian*).

In the sixth lesson, we will be looking at social meanings of *ain't* specifically through the lens of dictionary definitions. This lesson will complete our work on *ain't* and set up some of our later, more detailed work with dictionaries. For this short lesson, students will be comparing definitions and labels—whether dialect, nonstandard, substandard, colloquial, or slang. As I noted above, when the 1961 edition of Webster's included *ain't* and didn't label it as pejoratively as some thought it should be, there was a flood of criticism. Richard Bailey (1995) describes the controversy in a review of *The Story of Webster's Third*:

> "*Ain't* ain't a word 'cause it ain't in the dictionary" is a folk adage commonly quoted to me by my students, and their credulous acceptance of it illustrates their conviction that dictionaries regulate English and that words not appearing in them aren't words. It also suggests that they have never bothered to look up *ain't* in a dictionary.
>
> Though attested in print only from the late 18th century, *ain't* became a shibboleth [a language feature that distinguishes "good speakers" from "bad speakers"] in the 19th and was regularly treated as such by lexicographers, not only in the *Oxford English Dictionary* but also in large American dictionaries for general use, for instance *The New Century* (1927; "vulgar") and the second edition of the *Merriam-Webster New International* (1934; "dial. or ill."). The treatment of *ain't* in Philip Gove's third edition of the *New International* (1961; "though disapproved by many and more common in less educated speech, used orally in most parts of the U.S. by many cultivated speakers") created a firestorm of criticism and a vigorous assault on "structural linguistics." (604)

The ways that dictionaries label words obviously carry a lot of weight and both reflect and influence how people think about those words. It is useful, therefore, to interrogate these labels. During this process, students will also practice argumentation and get some preliminary experience working with dictionaries.

ONLINE RESOURCES

Ain't Misbehavin'
www.ischool.berkeley.edu/
~nunberg/aint.html

lesson plan 6 <u>Ain't</u> in the Dictionary

MATERIALS

Copies of Handout 6:1

OTHER IDEAS

This last exercise might be a good opportunity for students to practice close reading and writing analytical paragraphs. You may want to give them additional time to write and, perhaps, edit their responses.

Objectives

- Students will become acquainted with some features of dictionaries.
- Students will practice critical analysis by examining some basic labeling in dictionary definitions.
- Students will practice writing analytical paragraphs.

Procedures

1. Tell students that they will look at how *ain't* is defined in dictionaries. Ask students, "Who writes definitions in dictionaries?" (It is not necessary to go into too much detail here, as we are going to be revisiting these questions later. However, students should, at least, understand that dictionaries are made by people, and those people make choices about how words are represented and labeled.)
2. Distribute Handout 6:1 and review the definitions for A and B.
3. Answer the questions in Part I as a class. These may be fairly difficult questions. Feel free to give students as much guidance and framing as they need.
4. Review the directions for Part II and have students answer the questions individually or in small groups. Review and collect their responses.

ANSWER KEY

Handout 6:1

Part I

1. The first part of the first question (what is missing from the definitions?) should be fairly straightforward. Why it's not included is more difficult to answer—perhaps because it's less common, perhaps because it's more specifically a feature of African American English. It's not necessary for students to arrive at a particular answer. It's more important for them to think carefully about the question.
2. The second question might be somewhat easier: *substandard* is decidedly more negative than *nonstandard*. But this question will also force students to think a bit about what *standard* means. This is an issue we will engage in greater detail in the next lesson.

Part II

Answers will certainly vary, but some points of interest may be the claim of stupidity or intentionality in the first definition, the assertion that *ain't* isn't in the dictionary in the second, and the labeling of *ain't* as slang in the third.

Handout 6:1 **Ain't** in the Dictionary

Below are two definitions for *ain't* from different dictionaries. Review the definitions and answer the questions for Part I as a class. Then, follow your teacher's instructions for Part II.

> A. *The American Heritage Dictionary of the English Language: Fourth Edition*
> *Nonstandard* 1. Contraction of *am not*. 2. Used also as a contraction for *are not, is not, has not,* and *have not.*

> B. *Webster's Ninth New Collegiate Dictionary*
> 1. a: are not b: is not c: am not 2. *substand* a: have not b: has not

Part I
Discuss the following two questions as a class.

1. Based on our work on what *ain't* can stand for, what is missing from these definitions? Why do think it's not included in the definitions?
2. What is the difference between labeling *ain't* "nonstandard" (A) and "substandard" (B)?

Part II
The following definitions for *ain't* appear in an online dictionary (Urban Dictionary).

> A. Nonsense word substituted for "isn't" mainly used by four groups of people: (1) Ignoramuses. (2) People who want to pretend to be ignorant to fit in. (3) Songwriters who need to cut out a syllable. (4) Kids who want to annoy their parents or teachers.

> B. A form of saying is not, are not. This is a word people should not use because it is not actually a word defined by the dictionary. If you use it, it shows that you are not an educated person.

> C. Slang contraction of is not, are not, am not, do not or does not.

Choose one of the three definitions and write a paragraph responding to it. Your paragraph should answer these three questions.
1. Is the definition complete and accurate?
2. How is *ain't* being labeled?
3. What is your response to how *ain't* is being labeled?

"Using formal English is not the same as using Standard English. 'Formal' describes a range of registers, while 'Standard' describes a particular dialect of English; one can use formal registers in Vernacular as well as Standard English."

What Is Standard English?

Key Points

- What counts as Standard English has changed over time.
- Spoken and written standards are different and change at different rates.
- Some features are more marked as Vernacular than others.
- Code-switching is not the same thing as register- or style-switching. When people are being more "formal," therefore, they are not necessarily being more or less Standard.

Background for Teachers

Most of us have a sense that there is a thing that we call "Standard English"—we have, after all, been using the term in these materials as if it were something on which everyone agreed. However, actually defining Standard English is a little more complicated than it might seem. The two complications I want to address here are the differences between written and spoken language and the differences between dialect and register, which crucially distinguishes formal from standard language.

Written and spoken language are distinct. Written language can be endlessly scrutinized and edited and, therefore, is more easily compared from text to text and normalized. Spoken language, however, is more ephemeral and much of the time, we are not conscious of precisely how other people, or even we ourselves, talk. The pace of change is, then, different for written and spoken English as is the stability of what we understand to be "standard." Let's consider what constitutes the spoken standard and the written standard separately.

Part of what is perceived as spoken Standard English is influenced by grammatical features. For example, verb forms, noun forms, and pronouns can all play a part in marking a dialect as either Standard or Vernacular. Not all such features, however, are perceived equally. The use of *ain't*, as we have seen, is a feature strongly marked as Vernacular. A similarly marked feature is multiple negation. Multiple negation was once common in English. Some of the most revered authors in the English language like Chaucer and Shakespeare were frequent users of multiple negation. In *As You Like It*, Celia says, "I cannot goe no further . . ." and in *Hamlet*, Hamlet tells the players, "Nor do not saw the air too much with your hand, thus . . ." However, in the eighteenth century, mathematical logic was applied to language and multiple negation was warned against.

> But the two negatives as used by the Saxons and French must be understood by way of apposition . . . which way of speaking is still in use among us; and in this case the two negatives answer to the addition of two negative quantities in Algebra, the sum of which is negative. But our ordinary use of two negatives (in which the force of the first is much more than merely destroyed by the latter) corresponds to the multiplication of two negative quantities in Algebra, the product of which is affirmative; as mathematicians very well know. (Benjamin Martin, 1748)

Despite the apparent arbitrariness of such pronouncements and to the disappointment of some (in 1873, Fitzedward Hall lamented, "The double negative has been abandoned, to the great injury of strength of expression"), multiple negation has become strongly marked as nonstandard usage.

But other features often regarded as Standard are not as strongly marked as we might think. Consider the relative pronouns *who* and *whom*. We are probably inclined to think of *who* as being the subject pronoun ("And indeed nothing is easier for a man **who** has, as the phrase goes, 'followed the sea' with reverence and affection") and *whom* as being the object ("The idleness of a passenger, my isolation amongst all these men with **whom** I had no point of contact") in Standard English, as the vast majority of usage guides advise. This is certainly the case in written English, but is it in spoken English? In truth, almost all English speakers, even those who speak varieties considered Standard, are prone to using *who* as both subject and object pronoun. When speaking extemporaneously, both a president and a former network news anchor are users of *who* as object:

> And personal accounts will enable a worker to be able to pass on his or her earnings to **whoever** he or she chooses . . . (George W. Bush in a 2005 press conference)

> And unfortunately, there are few people in that corporate environment, virtually none **who** I can cite on any network . . . (Walter Cronkite in a 1999 *Frontline* interview)

These quotations are not so much evidence that people make mistakes when they speak, but rather that the use of *who* in the objective case is not a particularly marked feature of the spoken standard. (That the subjective and objective case would collapse in this way is not surprising because all English nouns used to have different endings marking them as subject or object, and the only surviving vestiges of that system are pronouns.) What is relevant to our discussion here is that some features like *ain't* and multiple negation are strongly marked as Vernacular, and others like the use of *who* are not. The grammatical markers of the spoken standard, then, are not fixed and consistent.

An additional complication arises when trying to define Standard English for spoken language because perceptions of what is standard are influenced not only by grammar but also by accent. Is there a Standard English accent? Some might consider the "accentless" speech of news anchors to be representative of the standard. No speech, however, is truly "accentless." The intensity of an accent is a matter of perception and familiarity. Compare the voices of a broadcaster from a 1940s newsreel to that of a current anchor on a network newscast. Others contend that the standard accent is simply the accent of the economically and politically powerful. But such accents are hardly homogeneous and change with time. Just listen to Franklin Roosevelt. Would we, today, consider his East Coast patrician accent to be standard?

Defining Standard English for written language is a little easier than doing so for spoken language, but there are still ambiguities. As I noted in the book's introduction, written language has registers—it varies according use. For some uses like journalism and academic writing, it might be relatively easy to conclude that, though they may be in different registers, still primarily use Standard English. But what about other uses, say for blogs or MySpace pages? Are those registers still a part of the standard dialect?

The range of registers available to all dialects, whether Standard or Vernacular, raises an important issue: **switching between registers is not the same as switching between dialects.** Switching between dialects—what is often called *code-switching*—requires changing systematic grammatical features, like changing verb or pronoun patterns.[4] Changing registers is often marked by the application of specific vocabularies. Registers can have preferred grammatical features, say a preference for subordination versus coordination. But note that attending to a register feature is different from code-switching; a speaker can subordinate or coordinate, for example, in any variety of English.

IMPORTANT TERMS

accent: The systematic pronunciation of a dialect.

One factor influencing accent is where in the mouth vowels are articulated. Do *pin* and *pen* sound the same when you say them? What about the vowel in *dude*? Is the vowel pronounced in very back of your mouth or more toward the front? Another factor influencing accent is the articulation of consonants. How do you pronounce *-ing*? Does the tip of your tongue hit the ridge just behind your teeth, or does the back of your tongue touch against the back of your mouth? Finally, accent is influenced by the tonal rise and fall and inflections of speech.

One important implication of this difference is that using formal English is not the same as using Standard English. "Formal" describes a range of registers, while "Standard" describes a particular dialect of English; one can use formal registers in Vernacular as well as Standard English. Here, for example, is an excerpt from a sermon.

> Those of you who know Brother Young know what a wonderful man he is, and he just came in and made **hisself** at home, and every time that I see him, he never fails to mention that night.[5]

In general, church is a social context that calls for more formal language, and the formality of the excerpt is unmistakable. Yet, the minister, as a speaker of Appalachian English, uses a pronoun system that is different from Standard English (*hisself* vs. *himself*). In his sermon, then, the minister uses a Vernacular dialect and a formal register.

Academic writing requires fluency in both a dialect (Standard English) and in registers (formal, academic registers). Students might have difficulty, for example, if they were using a formal register of a Vernacular dialect and were confident they were meeting the expectations for language in school. In coming to an understanding of Standard English, therefore, it is important for students to explore this crucial distinction.

ONLINE RESOURCES

Why "Standard" English
www.wonderfulwritingskills unhandbook.com/html/ standard/english

Three Views of Standard English
www.phon.ucl.ac.uk/home/ dick/standard.htm

The Sounds of Spoken Language
www.uiowa.edu/~acadtech/ phonetics/

American Tongues
www.cnam.com/ videoclips/American Tongues/tongues_ videomain.htm

lesson plan 7   What is Formal English?

MATERIALS

Copies of Handout 7:1

OTHER IDEAS

Because students may find the list of words to be dated, you might start with the list of four situations and have students generate their own lists of words. Even more challenging, they could generate lists of synonyms. You could, then, ask students if under any circumstances a word from one context might be used in another.

ANSWER KEY

Handout 7:1

Answers, of course, will vary. Students may well contend that they don't use any of these words with their friends. Because popular youth slang tends to change very quickly, and because many of these words have already passed into the mainstream vocabulary, they may find these words to be too dated. Still, they may find most of these words to be informal.

Objectives

- Students will investigate whether certain words are formal or informal.
- Through this exercise, students will begin defining Standard English.

Procedures

1. Remind students that in the last lesson they looked at how *ain't* was labeled in dictionaries. One label that was applied to *ain't* was "nonstandard." Now, in the next two lessons, we want to investigate what that, and its counterpart "standard," means. Before we talk about what standard language is, however, we want to talk about the difference between formal and informal language. Then we can work on distinguishing formal language from standard language.

2. Here we would like to have a brief discussion with students about how our language changes when we are in different social situations. The metaphor of clothing might be useful: In some situations we dress up our language; in others we might dress it down. Almost all people adjust their language—as they adjust their attire—to fit their social surroundings. Most of us wouldn't wear a tux or a gown to ballgame any more than we would ask the vendor at the park for a *saucisson* (or even a *frankfurter*?) when we wanted a hot dog.

3. Distribute Handout 7:1.

4. Have students complete Handout 7:1 individually, in small groups, or as a whole class.

5. Review their responses. You might ask students why they would expect to hear particular words in particular settings. The objective is to get students thinking and talking about relative levels of formality. Collect their work.

Handout 7:1 # What Is Formal English?

Answer the questions that follow the list of words below.

A. Bling
    It was a positive track but he went in another direction and started **bling blingin'** and everything else. (Don Cannon in *Concrete* interview)
B. Google
    They **Googled** him and then went onto a website. (Mike Carey in BBC interview)
C. Played (out)
    I never lost my swagger anyway although the industry has tried to tell us that our style is **played out**. (DJ Premier in *Plastic Soup* interview by Jimmy Coultas)
D. Cool
    Our team's too **cool**. (*Bring It On*)
E. Like
    This weekend he called me up and he's all "Where were you today?" and I'm **like** "I'm at my Grandmother's house." (*Clueless*)
F. Dis
    Ain't nobody **dissed** or dismissed me, Derek. (*Save the Last Dance*)

List those words from the above list that you think you would likely:

1. hear talking with friends

2. hear on the radio

3. read in a newspaper

4. use in a paper for school

lesson plan 8

What Is Formal English? Continued

MATERIALS

Copies of Handout 8:1

OTHER IDEAS

You might look at a more sustained piece of nonfiction like Rebecca Walker's "Before Hip-Hop Was Hip-Hop" (www. rebecca walker.com/essay_ 2005_before-hip-hop.htm) and analyze its use of formal versus informal language. Or have students go online and collect examples from newspapers of "informal" language—language that they don't think that they can use in their academic writing.

ANSWER KEY

Handout 8:1

Question 1
Answers will vary. Students may be surprised to see these words in these contexts, but probably not. These are excerpted from feature articles, which are more tolerant of informal language as stylistic devices than news articles. Also, these words, although relatively new, have had long enough lives as slang to enter the popular vocabulary. These are words most people know, even if they don't use them.

Question 2
We may not know for certain why these writers chose these words, but they are certainly conscious stylistic choices. In A, bling-bling is meant to convey something about the flashy character of the cars. In B, the writer may be trying to echo the language of music lyrics in the review.

Objectives

• Students will investigate whether certain words are formal or informal.

• Through this exercise, students will begin defining Standard English.

Procedures

1. Remind students that they will continue their discussion of formal versus informal language.

2. Distribute Handout 8:1.

3. Have students complete Handout 8:1 individually, in small groups, or as a whole class. These quotations raise the issue of using informal language in formal writing. Who gets to play with language in this way and why? These two quotations are excerpted from feature articles. Would a news article use language like this? What about an editorial? Can students use informal language in academic writing? Most of the time, probably not, but why?

4. Review students' responses.

Handout 8:1 # What Is Formal English?
Continued

Each of the quotations below comes from publications that most people associate with formal language. Read the quotations and answer the questions that follow.

A. Chrysler is threatening G.M.'s reign as king of the trend-setting **bling-bling** cars and trucks. (Hakim, *New York Times*)

B. His **dis** of one hopeful's off-key song. (Chu, *Time Magazine*)

1. Does it surprise you to see these words used in these publications? Why or why not?

2. Why do you think the writers chose to use these particular words?

lesson plan **9**   Code-Switching Using <u>Ain't</u>

MATERIALS

Copies of Handout 9:1

OTHER IDEAS

If you are interested in doing some additional technical work on verb tenses and aspects, this may be a natural time to talk about the present and past perfect. What are they and how are they formed? The perfect aspect indicates the relationship between a previous state or action and one occurring at a later time. In Standard English, the past, present, and future forms of the perfect aspect combine the appropriate form of *have* with a main verb (V + -*ed/en,* or what's commonly called the past participle), like, for example, *have written, had called,* or *will have finished.* Can students recognize the main verb in 4, 5, and 6 of the handout?

ANSWER KEY

Handout 9:1

Part I
1. are not
2. ain't
3. is not
   Rule X: ain't
   Rule Y: am not, are not (aren't), is not (isn't)

Part II
4. has not
5. ain't
6. have not
   Rule X: ain't
   Rule Y: has not (hasn't), have not (haven't)

Objectives

- Students will begin defining Standard English.
- Students will begin comparing the features of Standard and Vernacular English.

Procedures

1. Tell students that we've looked at formal and informal language. Now we want to compare Standard and Vernacular language. We're going to start by revisiting the work we've already done with *ain't.*

2. Distribute Handout 9:1 and review the directions with the students. It might be productive at this point in the unit to introduce *code-switching* to the students as a term. You might tell students that we're going to start comparing features of Standard and Vernacular English. This is a little different from comparing formal and informal language, which we just did. As we saw in the *New York Times* and *Time Magazine* quotations, you can be informal but still be using Standard English, just as you can be formal and use Vernacular English or slang. Adjusting your language to be more or less formal is called *style-switching;* moving between Standard and Vernacular English is called *code-switching.* At the moment, this may be a little confusing, but it should become clearer as we go along. We've already done some work comparing Standard and Vernacular English when we looked at *ain't.* Now we want to reinforce what we know, then extend our knowledge to other comparisons.

3. As a class, complete the rule and have the students write it on the handout. Having worked with *ain't* already, this shouldn't take too much time.

Handout 9:1 # Code-Switching Using <u>Ain't</u>

For each of the following pairs, fill in the blank with the missing form. If the Vernacular form is given, provide the Standard equivalent, and if the Standard is given, provide the Vernacular. Then complete the rules that begin at the bottom.

	System X = Vernacular	System Y = Standard
1.	Humph! Y'all let her worry yuh. You <u>ain't</u> like me. (*Their Eyes Were Watching God* by Zora Neale Hurston)	You _____ like me.
2.	I _____ afraid . . .	My citing the creation of tension as part of the work of the nonviolent-resister may sound rather shocking. But I must confess that I <u>am not</u> afraid of the word "tension." ("Letter from a Birmingham Jail" by Dr. Martin Luther King, Jr.)
3.	Well, they can just take they stocking down 'cause it <u>ain't</u> Christmas . . . (*The Bluest Eye* by Toni Morrison)	. . . it _____ Christmas.
Rule X: In some Vernacular varieties, the negative form of *to be* in the present tense is/are:		**Rule Y:** In Standard English, the negative form of *to be* in the present tense is/are:

	System X = Vernacular	System Y = Standard
4.	Scout yonder's been readin' ever since she was born, and she <u>ain't</u> even started to school yet. (*To Kill a Mockingbird* by Harper Lee)	. . . she _____ even started . . .
5.	I _____ said . . .	So I <u>have not</u> said to my people: "Get rid of your discontent." ("Letter from a Birmingham Jail" by Dr. Martin Luther King, Jr.)
6.	I don't want all that loud carrying on around here. I'm surprised you <u>ain't</u> woke Maretha up. (*The Piano Lesson* by August Wilson)	. . . you _____ woken . . .
Rule X: In some Vernacular varieties, the negative form of the auxiliary verb in the **present perfect** is/are:		**Rule Y:** In Standard English, the negative form of the auxiliary verb in the **present perfect** is/are:

lesson plan **10** Code Switching Using Predicative Adjectives

MATERIALS

Copies of Handout 10:1

IMPORTANT TERMS

predicative adjective: An adjective joined to the noun that it modifies by a linking verb (as opposed to an attributive adjective, which usually precedes the noun that it modifies).

zero copula: A grammatical construction in which the linking (or so-called *copular*) verb between the subject and predicate is implied, rather than explicitly stated.

On Handout 10:1 you will find a number of zero copula constructions with predicative adjectives. The zero copula can also be used with predicative nouns: "You a horrible-looking chick at this hour" (*A Raisin in the Sun* by Lorraine Hansberry). Note that the linking verb can be absent only in the present tense (*is, are*) and that the linking verb (*am*) must be there in the first person singular. Other languages that have a zero copula include Russian and Hebrew.

ANSWER KEY

Handout 10:1

1. are mad
2. is here
3. 'm just sleepy (answer provided)
4. is just tired
5. am cognizant (or 'm cognizant)

Rule X: nothing; (with the exception of) the first-person singular (*I*)

Rule Y: the verb to be (*are, is, am*)

Objectives

* Students will continue defining Standard English.
* Students will begin recognizing sentence subjects.
* Students will compare the how predicative adjectives are structured in Standard and Vernacular English.

Procedures

1. Remind students that they will again compare Standard and Vernacular English.
2. Distribute Handout 10:1.
3. Review the directions with the students. Although it's important to expose students to some technical vocabulary here, it's not important that they memorize what a predicative adjective is, for example. Rather, they should simply recognize this as a common type of sentence. Also, predicate adjectives are sometimes referred to as *subject complements*. If you are more comfortable with that term, you can use it as a substitute.
4. Have students complete Handout 10:1 either individually or in small groups.
5. Review students' responses in class. The implied *to be* in this kind of construction is called a *zero copula*. Note that this construction only works in the present tense and that in the first-person singular, the verb must be there. The forms that can be implied, then, are *is* and *are*.
6. At the conclusion of the lesson, you might discuss with students what they think the difference is between formal English and Standard English. Formal English is marked largely, though not exclusively, by vocabulary. Standard English is marked by specific grammatical forms. Students certainly would not be expected to condense these complex ideas to definitions like these; however, they might touch on similar ideas. If they don't have a definitive answer, that's okay. This will be an ongoing topic of discussion.

OTHER IDEAS

In this exercise, the predictive adjective follows the verb *to be*. Predicative adjectives, however, can follow other verbs as well. Can students come up with other examples like *seem, appear*, and so on? What properties does such verbs share?

Handout 10:1 # Code-Switching Using Predicative Adjectives

In one common type of sentence, we have a subject and want to describe it some way.

A.

She	was	invisible
subject		predicative adjective

B.

She	's	way past forty
subject		predicative adjective

Notice that in this type of sentence, the adjective comes at the end of sentence rather than next to the noun. The predicative adjective can be a single word (as in A) or a group of words that works like an adjective (as in B).

In some Vernacular varieties of English, these kinds of sentences are formed differently from Standard English. For each of the following pairs, fill in the blank with the missing form. If the Vernacular form is given, provide the Standard equivalent, and if the Standard is given, provide the Vernacular. Then complete the rules that begin at the bottom. Note that the person and number of the pronoun is listed in the left-hand column (for example, 2nd per. sing. = *you*). Note, also, that #3 has been done for you. This clue will help you complete the table and the rule.

	System X: Vernacular	System Y: Standard
1. (2nd per. sing.)	You mean, <u>you mad</u> 'cause she didn't stop and tell us all her business. (*Their Eyes Were Watching God* by Zora Neale Hurston)	. . . you _____ 'cause . . .
2. (3rd per. sing.)	"Fuller?" The name was familiar to the man's tongue. "I don't know, <u>he here</u> somewhere . . ." (*The Bluest Eye* by Toni Morrison)	. . . he _____ somewhere . . .
3. (1st per. sing.)	No—<u>I'm just sleepy</u> as the devil. (*A Raisin in the Sun* by Lorraine Hansberry)	. . . <u>I'm just sleepy</u> as . . .
4. (3rd per. sing.)	No—<u>she just tired</u>. She was out this evening. (*A Raisin in the Sun* by Lorraine Hansberry)	. . . she _____. She was . . .
5. (1st per. sing.)	. . . I _____ of . . .	Moreover, <u>I am cognizant</u> of the interrelatedness of all communities and states. ("Letter from a Birmingham Jail" by Dr. Martin Luther King, Jr.)
	Rule X: In some Vernacular varieties of English, a **subject** and a **predicative adjective** in the present tense are linked by: With the exception of:	**Rule Y:** In Standard English, a **subject** and a **predicative adjective** in the present tense are linked by:

Reflexive Pronouns

"These paradigms illustrate what we mean by grammatical rules: Both Standard and Vernacular dialects have a system governing reflexive pronouns."

Key Points

- A paradigm shows a word in all its inflected forms for both person (first, second, and third) and number (singular and plural).
- Pronoun paradigms have changed as English has evolved.
- Standard English merged its second-person singular and plural pronouns. Because of this gap, the second-person plural is a frequent place of innovation for Vernacular dialects.
- Reflexive pronouns refer back to the subject of a clause.
- Reflexive pronouns generally take the form of *possessive pronoun + self* (or *selves*).
- *Himself* and *themselves* are exceptions to the pattern in Standard English. They are *object pronoun + self.*
- In some Vernacular dialects, the pattern of *possessive pronoun + self* remains consistent, yielding *hisself* and *theirselves.*

Background for Teachers

English pronouns are a rich subject for investigation. As I noted in the background to the previous lessons on Standard English, pronouns are a link to our linguistic past. All nouns used to be marked for case. That is, the endings of nouns used to change depending on the noun's relationship to a verb or preposition (Old English nouns, in fact, could be in any of five different cases). For example, the Old English word for *stone*, *stān*, would be *stān* as the subject and *stāne* as the indirect object. In present day English, we still mark nouns for plurality (*-s* for regular nouns) and possession (*-'s*), but the only nouns that otherwise change are pronouns.

The systematic forms that pronouns take (for singular, plural, subject, object, and possession) can vary by dialect. One common form that varies is the second-person plural pronoun. Once, English differentiated the second-person singular pronoun, *pū* (thou), from the second person plural pronoun, *ġē* (ye), but both singular and plural merged into *you*. Because it is useful to be able to distinguish an individual from a group, many dialects have developed a second-person plural pronoun. Southern English uses the well-recognized *you all* or *y'all*; Pittsburghese uses *youns* or *yins*; and some dialects use *youse*. (Yet another variation is *you guys*.)

It is not only single pronouns that can differ, but also entire systems, or paradigms, that can vary. For example, English has two different kinds of possessive pronouns, dependent and independent. Dependent possessive pronouns modify nouns or noun phrases:

> If **my** children are silly I must hope to be always sensible of it . . .
> (*Pride and Prejudice* by Jane Austen)

Independent possessive pronouns can stand alone:

> This was a lucky idea of **mine**, indeed! (*Pride and Prejudice*)

In Standard English, the paradigm for independent possessive pronouns is as follows:

	Singular	**Plural**
First person	mine	ours
Second person	yours	yours
Third person	his/hers	theirs

Some Southern dialects, however, use a different paradigm.

	Singular	**Plural**
First person	mine(s)	ourn
Second person	yourn	y'alls(es)
Third person	hisn/hersn	theirn

This is a system that is sometimes evident in literature that uses Southern dialect features:

> But, Huck, dese kings o' **ourn** is reglar rapscallions. (*The Adventures of Huckleberry Finn*, Twain)

> Pheoby, dat Sam of **your'n** just won't quit! (*Their Eyes Were Watching God*, Hurston)

One thing that these kinds of paradigms reveal is that the use of Vernacular forms is not careless speech, but is, in fact, systematic; it's just a different system.

One paradigm that illustrates this systematicity particularly well is the one for reflexive pronouns. Reflexive pronouns most of the time refer back to the subject of the clause.

> Impossible, Mr. Bennet, impossible, when **I** am not acquainted with him **myself**. (*Pride and Prejudice*, Austen)

ONLINE RESOURCES

Hisself and Theirselves
color-connection.com/
EngVW/Lessons/lesson1.htm

In Standard English the paradigm for reflexive pronouns is as follows:

	Singular	Plural
First person	myself	ourselves
Second person	yourself	yourselves
Third person	himself/herself/itself	themselves

Notice that for the first and second person, the form takes the possessive form plus -*self*. The third person, however, takes objective form plus -*self*. Some dialects, however, keep possessive plus -*self* consistent throughout the paradigm.

	Singular	Plural
First person	myself	ourselves
Second person	yourself	yourselves
Third person	hisself/herself/itself	theirselves

In this particular instance, it is the Vernacular forms that appear more logically consistent than the standard ones. A related paradigm uses the possessive pronoun followed by the infix -*own*- followed by -*self*.

> Ah'll give one whole hawg **mah ownself**. (*Their Eyes Were Watching God*, Hurston)

It is useful for students to both puzzle out and see these paradigms for at least three reasons. First, these paradigms illustrate what we mean by grammatical rules: Both Standard and Vernacular dialects have a system governing reflexive pronouns. Second, in juxtaposing the two systems, students will practice code-switching . Third, attending to pronouns is a very important skill in both reading and writing. In fact, the effective use of pronouns can greatly enhance the coherence of students' essays. This lesson, then, will provide them a first foray into looking carefully at pronouns.

Objectives

- Students will be able to identify reflexive pronouns.
- Students' understanding of code-switching will increase by examining how reflexive pronoun systems work in Standard and Vernacular English.

Procedures

1. Remind students that we will continue to compare features of Standard and Vernacular English. Today we will compare reflexive pronoun systems. Here you may need to remind students what pronouns are, the person (first, second, and third), and number (singular or plural).
2. Distribute Handout 11:1 and review the directions with the students. You might point out to students that reflexive pronouns end in *-self* and usually refer back to the subject or topic of the sentence.
3. Have students complete Handout 11:1 either individually or in small groups.
4. Review their responses.
5. Now ask the class to answer the bonus question at the bottom of the page. If they are having difficulty, you might ask them to identify the differences between the two paradigms. This should be a quick identification of *himself* versus *hisself* and *themselves* versus *theirselves*. You can also direct students to the Help! column on their handout.

MATERIALS

Copies of Handout 11:1

ANSWER KEY

Handout 11:1

1. (answer provided)
2. myself
3. yourself/yourselves
4. itself
5. themselves
6. himself
7. ourselves

Vernacular Rule

	SINGULAR	PLURAL
1st	myself	ourselves
2nd	yourself	yourselves
3rd	hisself herself itself	theirselves

Standard Rule

	SINGULAR	PLURAL
1st	myself	ourselves
2nd	yourself	yourselves
3rd	himself herself itself	themselves

Bonus Question

Reflexive pronouns are formed by *possessive pronoun + self* (or *selves*) in some Vernacular varieties of English. They are formed the same way in Standard English except for *himself* and *themselves*, which are *object pronoun + self.*

Handout 11:1 Code-Switching Using Reflexive Pronouns

Both sets of quotations are from *Their Eyes Were Watching God* by Zora Neale Hurston. The first set is taken from dialogue, which uses Vernacular English. The second is taken from narration, which uses Standard English.

For each of the following pairs, fill in the blank with the missing reflexive pronoun. If the Vernacular form is given, provide the Standard equivalent, and if the Standard is given, provide the Vernacular. Then complete the rule that begins on the next page. You may standardize spelling for the Vernacular pronouns, so *yo'* would be *your* and *mah* would be *my*, for example.

System X: Vernacular	System Y: Standard
1. She asted me dat maybe twenty-five or thirty times, lak she got tuh sayin' dat and couldn't help <u>herself</u>.	She took careful stock of <u>herself</u>, then combed her hair and tied it back up again.
2. Ah couldn't love yuh no more if Ah had uh felt yo' birth pains <u>mahself</u>.	. . . your birth pains _____.
3. Neither can you stand alone by <u>yo'self</u>.	. . . by _____. *What if the speaker were talking to a group of people? Neither can y'all stand alone by _____.
4. It connected _____ with . . .	It connected <u>itself</u> with other vaguely felt matters that had struck her outside observation and buried themselves in her flesh.
5. He had always wanted to be a big voice, but de white folks had all de sayso where he come from and everywhere else, exceptin' dis place dat colored folks was buildin' <u>theirselves</u>.	. . . was building _____.
6. Now, Lum, you know dat mule ain't aimin' tuh let <u>hisself</u> be caught.	. . . to let _____ be caught.
7. Even if dey don't take us in wid de whites, dey oughta make us uh class tuh <u>ourselves</u>.	. . . a class to _____.

Instead of writing out the rules in sentences, you will be filling out paradigms. A paradigm is just a chart that gives the form of a pronoun or verb for each person (first, second, or third) and number (singular or plural).

The reflexive pronoun paradigms of some Vernacular varieties of English are different from Standard English. In each of the boxes, write in the reflexive pronoun or pronouns for the correct case and number. You can refer to the exercise that you just completed from *Their Eyes Were Watching God.* For the first-person singular, for example, look at #2.

Rule for Reflexive Pronouns in Vernacular English

	SINGULAR	PLURAL
First person (I, we)		
Second person (you)		
Third person (he, she, it, they)		

Rule for Reflexive Pronouns in Standard English

	SINGULAR	PLURAL
First person (I, we)		
Second person (you)		
Third person (he, she, it, they)		

Bonus Question

Reflexive pronouns are formed by adding *-self* or *-selves* to what in Vernacular English? In Standard English? (If you need a hint, look at the paradigms in the Help! column.) Which is a more consistent paradigm, the Vernacular or the Standard? Can you explain?

 help!

Here are some examples of paradigms.

The verb *to be* in the present tense:

	SINGULAR	PLURAL
1st	am	are
2nd	are	are
3rd	is	are

Object pronouns (pronouns that are the targets of verbs or prepositions; the underlined pronouns, for example, in "No one told <u>me</u> about <u>her</u>"):

	SINGULAR	PLURAL
1st	me	us
2nd	you	you
3rd	him her it	them

Possessive pronouns (pronouns that show possession come before a noun; the underlined pronoun, for example, in "None of <u>your</u> business"):

	SINGULAR	PLURAL
1st	my	our
2nd	your	your
3rd	his her its	their

"According to Schoolhouse Rock!, 'A noun's a special kind of word / It's any name you ever heard / I find it quite interest-ing / A noun's a person, place or thing.' This is a handy rule of thumb that most of us have learned at one time and that covers many nouns, but, in many ways, it is incomplete, even confusing."

Dictionaries

Key Points

- Dictionaries can provide important information about words, their usage, and their origins.
- The content of dictionaries, although reliable, is the product of many choices and, thus, is not absolute.
- In order to determine a word's part of speech, we need to distinguish its form from its function.

Background for Teachers

In Lesson 6, students were introduced to some of the choices that go into the making of dictionaries. Now we want to look at dictionary entries in a little more detail and give students an opportunity to draft some dictionary entries of their own. The analysis and composition of dictionary entries will provide a useful platform for working with parts of speech and wrestling with some even more complex word categories like transitive versus intransitive and regular versus irregular verbs.

   We tend to think of dictionaries as authoritative and rather unambiguous. It is the place, after all, that most of us turn when we want to find out what a word

Important Terms

noun: By function, a noun is a word that can be the subject or object of a verb. By form, a most nouns can be preceded by an article (*a/an/the*). Also, in Standard English, most regular nouns can accept the plural marker *-s* and the possessive marker *-'s*.

verb: By function, a verb is a word that can accept a subject. By form, verbs can be marked for time (like past time, for example, by adding *-ed* to regular verbs in Standard English). Also, in Standard English, most verbs can accept the third-person singular marker *-s* in present (nonpast) time.

Note: Some verbs require a direct object, and others do not. Whether or not a verb needs a direct object determines its transitivity. A transitive verb needs a direct object, and an intransitive verb does not.

means. But dictionaries, of course, are made by people. And as such, they are subject to various motivations and decision-making processes. At different times, they have been viewed as preservers of the English language, bulwarks against moral and intellectual decline as well as authentication of national identity. In addition to the assorted values motivating their creation, dictionaries are subject to a host of editorial choices. What words are included? When, for example, should *google* be put in (as Webster's now has) and when should a word like *manutenency* (meaning the act of holding or support) be taken out? And how should words be labeled? Should *google* be labeled "slang"? (We encountered some of the complications of labeling words with *ain't*.) Furthermore, how are definitions composed? What definitions are included? And how are definitions ordered?

In addition to engaging questions about existing dictionary definitions, students will be given the opportunity to compose entries themselves. The composition of entries will foster students' role as informants about their language use. The entries will also force students to think through how words function as parts of speech.

It isn't always straightforward determining what part of speech a word is. How, for example, do we recognize nouns? According to *Schoolhouse Rock!*, "A noun's a special kind of word / It's any name you ever heard / I find it quite interesting / A noun's a person, place or thing." This is a handy rule of thumb that most of us have learned at one time and that covers many nouns, but, in many ways, it is incomplete, even confusing. What, for example, about actions like *running* or *thinking*? Certainly, such actions can function as nouns:

> . . . to talk to each other is but a more animated and an audible **thinking**. (*Jane Eyre* by Charlotte Brontë)

In addition, a person, place, or thing isn't always unambiguously a noun. Consider the word *Sacramento*. A proper noun, right? What about in the following sentence?

> It looked very much like it was going to be a **Sacramento** sweep, over on Sunday in Game 3 at Arco Arena. (Voepel, ESPN)

In this example, we might conclude that *Sacramento* is functioning as an adjective (modifying *sweep*) rather than as a noun. However, an important characteristic of an adjective is that it has comparative and superlative forms, either by adding the suffixes *-er* and *-est* or the adverbs *more* and *most*. By this test, *Sacramento* is not an adjective; the sweep cannot be *more Sacramento*.

In determining parts of speech, then, we might think about form versus function. For example, by function, a noun is a word that can be the subject or object of a verb. What, then, is the part of speech of *Boston* in the following example?

> A **Boston** sweep would effectively eliminate the Yankees from the division race by Sunday night. (Feinsand, *New York Daily News*)

IMPORTANT TERMS

adjective: By function, an adjective modifies a noun. By form, an adjective can have comparative and superlative forms, either by adding the suffixes *-er* and *-est* or the adverbs *more* and *most.*

As I have noted, words that normally function as other parts of speech (like nouns) can sometimes function as adjectives. At other times, however, an adjective can be formed by adding a suffix to a word stem. On Handout 13:3, there is a partial list of adjectival suffixes. One of the most productive suffixes on the list is one of the simplest, *-y.* It is also interesting to note that these suffixes do not always follow our expectations. Why, for example, is *awful* an antonym and not a synonym for *awesome*?

ONLINE RESOURCES

Dictionaries and Meanings
www.bl.uk/learning/langlit/
dic/meanings.html

**Some Quotes About
Dictionaries**
http://faculty.fortlewis.edu/
BENZ_B/engl461/
dictionaries.html

Reading a Dictionary Entry
www.cabrillo.edu/services
/writingcenter/290/
dictionary3.html

Boston is part of the phrase *A Boston sweep* that serves as the subject of the verb *would eliminate.* But *sweep* is the root, the head, of that phrase. It's not "a Boston" but "a sweep" that threatens to eliminate the Yankees. *Boston* tells us what kind of sweep it is. *Boston* modifies *sweep.*

In order to determine whether or not *Boston* is a noun by form, there are a number of tests. One form test for nouns is that, in Standard English, they can take an article (the definite *the* or indefinite *a/an*). Proper names like *Boston* can cause problems because they don't usually take articles (unless you're *the* Donald or attend *the* Ohio State University). Another form test is that regular nouns, in Standard English, can accept the plural marker *-s.* With proper names like *Boston,* however, this test, like the first one, fails. (Nouns that can't be counted like *courage* or *education* also don't follow this rule.) Yet another test is that nouns, in Standard English, can accept the possessive marker *-'s. Boston* meets this test; we could have "Boston's sweep," for example. Thus, by form, *Boston* is unmistakably a noun, but in the example, it is functioning as an adjective.

In the lesson, students might run up against similar ambiguities with *dog.* They might, for example, generate uses like *dog tired* or *dog days.* In the first case, the argument could be made that *dog* is an adverb modifying *tired* and in the second it is an adjective modifying *days.* In both cases, however, *dog* by form is unambiguously a noun; it is its function that changes.

Dictionaries, generally, identify the part of speech of a word by form. When students compose their own dictionary entries, they will do the same. It is still extraordinarily useful, however, for them to think about functions, as well. It will, for example, later be very useful for them to recognize a sentence subject like *a Boston sweep,* regardless of any disagreement on the identification of the individual words.

lesson plan **12** Reading Dictionaries

Objectives

- Students will practice identifying parts of speech.
- Students will become familiar with some of the features of dictionary entries.

Procedures

1. You might begin by engaging students in a general discussion about dictionaries. For what do we use dictionaries? Where do they come from? Who makes them? Are all words included in a dictionary? What words are left out? Why? Then, pass out and review Handout 12:1. (If you are pressed for time, you might begin with the handouts and let the previous questions emerge from analysis of the dictionary entry on Handout 12:2.)

2. Have students look at the definition for *dog* on Handout 12:2. Discuss the first three questions as a class and have students write down their responses. Students may or may not have some difficulty with the second question. If they have trouble responding, this is an opportunity to review some fundamentals about parts of speech. You might start by pointing out that we're looking for a use of *dog* that is not a noun, and then asking, "What is a noun? How do we know when a word is a noun?" Here it might be useful to move away from the Schoolhouse Rock–type definition and introduce (even brainstorm) some of the form tests for nouns.

3. As a class, in pairs, or individually, have the students complete question 4.

4. Review and collect their responses.

MATERIALS

Copies of Handouts 12:1 and 12:2

ANSWER KEY

Handout 12:2

1. noun.
2. *Dog* can be a verb.
3. As a verb, it can mean *to pursue* ("He dogged her for a date"), *to loaf* ("The class dogged it during P.E."), among other things. Students may well have their own definitions.
4. For A, students will have a variety of answers. One widespread definition that is missing is *friend*. For B, students may want to eliminate some definitions and add others. Students may also want to reorder the definitions. It is a common assumption that definitions are ordered by popularity. Most dictionaries, however, do not rank definitions in this way.

Handout 12:1 # Reading Dictionaries

Below are explanations of some of the common features of dictionaries.

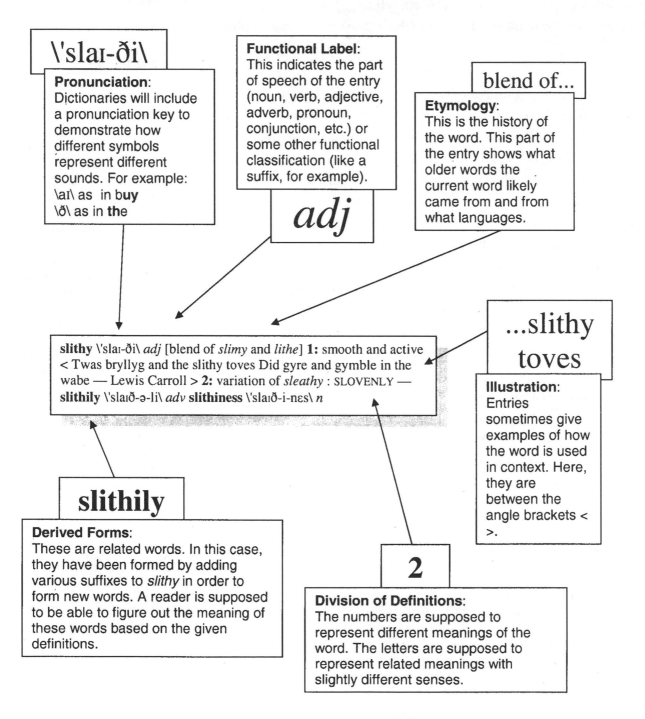

\'slaɪ-ði\

Pronunciation:
Dictionaries will include a pronunciation key to demonstrate how different symbols represent different sounds. For example:
\aɪ\ as in **buy**
\ð\ as in **the**

Functional Label:
This indicates the part of speech of the entry (noun, verb, adjective, adverb, pronoun, conjunction, etc.) or some other functional classification (like a suffix, for example).

adj

blend of...

Etymology:
This is the history of the word. This part of the entry shows what older words the current word likely came from and from what languages.

slithy \'slaɪ-ði\ *adj* [blend of *slimy* and *lithe*] **1**: smooth and active < Twas bryllyg and the slithy toves Did gyre and gymble in the wabe — Lewis Carroll > **2**: variation of *sleathy* : SLOVENLY — **slithily** \'slaɪð-ə-li\ *adv* **slithiness** \'slaɪð-i-nɛs\ *n*

...slithy toves

Illustration:
Entries sometimes give examples of how the word is used in context. Here, they are between the angle brackets < >.

slithily

Derived Forms:
These are related words. In this case, they have been formed by adding various suffixes to *slithy* in order to form new words. A reader is supposed to be able to figure out the meaning of these words based on the given definitions.

2

Division of Definitions:
The numbers are supposed to represent different meanings of the word. The letters are supposed to represent related meanings with slightly different senses.

Handout 12:2 **Reading Dictionaries, Continued**

Below is an entry for *dog* (which appears in the *Merriam-Webster Online Dictionary*). Read the definition and answer the questions that follow.

> **dog** \'dog, 'däg\ *n* [Middle English, from Old English *docga*] **1 a:** canid; *especially* : a highly variable domestic mammal (*Canis familiaris*) closely related to the gray wolf **b:** a male dog; *also* : a male usually carnivorous mammal **2 a:** a worthless or contemptible person **b:** fellow, chap <a lazy *dog*> <you lucky *dog*> **3 a:** any of various usually simple mechanical devices for holding, gripping, or fastening that consist of a spike, bar, or hook **b:** andiron **4:** uncharacteristic or affected stylishness or dignity <put on the *dog*> **5** *capitalized* : either of the constellations Canis Major or Canis Minor **6** *plural* : feet **7** *plural* : ruin <going to the *dogs*> **8:** one inferior of its kind <the movie was a *dog*> : as **a:** an investment not worth its price **b:** an undesirable piece of merchandise **9:** an unattractive person; *especially* : an unattractive girl or woman **10:** hot dog

1. The definitions are all for what part of speech?

2. What is another part of speech that *dog* can be? Give an example of how *dog* can be used in this way.

3. Write a definition for the usage you identify in question 2.

4. You are the editor of the entry above for *dog*.
   A. Many young speakers use *dog* with their friends in a way not listed here. What definition would you add, if you could?

   B. What changes might you suggest for definition 9?

lesson plan 13   Reading and Writing Dictionaries

MATERIALS

Copies of Handouts 13:1 and 13:2 (Handout 13:3 is optional)

OTHER IDEAS

Rather than having students make up sample sentences for their words, you can have them take an *Oxford English Dictionary* (OED) approach and look for real-world examples of their words online. Working with suffixes can actually help students to write more effectively. The adjectival suffixes on Handout 13:3 are called *derivational*. By adding such a suffix to a word, you derive a new word that is a different part of speech. The ones listed on Handout 13:3 make adjectives out of nouns. But other suffixes change verbs to nouns (like -*ion*), nouns to verbs (like -*ize*), and so on. Having control over this process isn't trivial. It's actually part of an ancient rhetorical strategy called *polyptoton*, and it can help students' writing to be more organized and coherent.

ANSWER KEY

Handout 13:2

Depending on the students' age and where they live, the words that students choose to define will vary widely. As we've noted, identifying the part of speech can be a stumbling block, as can composing illustrative sentences.

Objectives

- Students will practice identifying parts of speech.
- Students will demonstrate their knowledge by drafting dictionary entries.

Procedures

1. Start by telling students that they will write their own dictionary entries, but first they will review some information about dictionaries.
2. Distribute copies of Handout 13:1, and review the information with students.
3. Distribute copies of Handout 13:2, and review the instructions as a class. The entries will be for words that they or their friends use and that other people might not know or understand. They might imagine if a new student came to school from a different part of the country, what sort of lingo would he or she need to know in order to fit in? Give them the directions for the assignment, which are as follows.
   - The students will each write entries for two words. In order to maximize the available time, you might have the students work in pairs.
   - Have the students compose entries for two different parts of speech. You can divide nouns, verbs, and adjectives among the students/pairs, so that one student/pair writes an entry for a noun and a verb, another for a verb and an adjective, and so on.
   - The words should be ones that are appropriate for school.
   - Each entry will include the word, the part of speech, the definition, and a sentence illustrating its use.
4. Before students proceed to drafting their entries, you might allow them the opportunity to brainstorm possible words either as a class or in small groups. This also might be a good opportunity to quickly review parts of speech and strategies for identifying what part of speech a word might be.
5. Give students sufficient time to draft their entries. The amount of class time you want to devote to the drafting of entries is up to you.

Handout 13:1 **Reading and Writing Dictionaries**

BACKGROUND FOR STUDENTS

When you want to know what a word means, where do you turn? Probably to a dictionary. After all, dictionaries are *the* place to find out the correct way to use a word. But who makes dictionaries? What words are included? When, for example, should *google* be put in (as Webster's now has) and when should a word like *manutenency* (meaning the act of holding or support) be taken out? And how should words be labeled? Should *google* be labeled "slang"? Furthermore, how are definitions created? What definitions are included? And how are definitions ordered? Dictionaries are the result of many choices.

You've already been asked to think about these kinds of questions, and now you get to create your own dictionary entries. You'll have to think not only about what words mean, but how and when they are used. Easy, right? Maybe not. . . . For example, it isn't always straightforward determining what part of speech a word is. How, for example, do we recognize nouns? Simple. If it's a person, place, or thing, it's a noun. But what about actions like *running* or *thinking*? Certainly, such actions can function as nouns.

> . . . to talk to each other is but a more animated and an audible **thinking**. (*Jane Eyre* by Charlotte Brontë)

In determining parts of speech, then, we can think about form versus function. For example, by function, a noun is a word that can be the subject or object of a verb. What, then, is the part of speech of *Boston* in the following example?

> A **Boston** sweep would effectively eliminate the Yankees from the division race by Sunday night. (Feinsand, *New York Daily News*)

Boston is part of the phrase *A Boston sweep* that serves as the subject of the verb *would eliminate*. But *sweep* is the root, the head, of that phrase. It's not "a Boston" but "a sweep" that threatens to eliminate the Yankees. *Boston* tells us what kind of sweep it is. *Boston* modifies *sweep*.

In order to determine whether or not *Boston* is a noun by form, there are a number of tests. One form test for nouns is that, in Standard English, they can take an article (*a*/*an*/*the*). Proper names like *Boston*, however, don't usually take articles (unless you're *the* Donald or attend *the* Ohio State University). Another form test is that regular nouns, in Standard English, can accept the plural marker *-s*. With proper names like *Boston*, however, this test, like the first one, fails. (Nouns that can't be counted like *courage* or *education* also don't follow this rule.) Yet another test is that nouns, in Standard English, can accept the possessive marker *-'s*. *Boston* meets this test; we could have "Boston's sweep," for example. Thus, by form, *Boston* is unmistakably a noun, but in the example, it is functioning as an adjective.

Maybe putting together a dictionary, then, isn't so simple, but considering how much authority we give them, it's worth looking at what they really tell us.

KEY POINTS

- Dictionaries can provide important information about words, their usage, and their origins.
- The content of dictionaries, although very reliable, is the product of many choices and, thus, is not absolute.
- In order to determine a word's part of speech, we need to distinguish its form from its function.

IMPORTANT TERMS

noun: By function, a noun is a word that can be the subject or object of a verb or the object of a preposition. By form, most nouns can be preceded by an article (*a/an/the*). Also, in Standard English, most regular nouns can accept the plural marker *-s* (when countable) and the possessive marker *-'s*.

verb: By function, a verb is a word that can accept a subject. It can also function as an imperative. By form, verbs can be marked for time (like past time, for example, by adding *-ed* for regular verbs in Standard English). Also, in Standard English, verbs can accept the third-person singular marker *-s* in present (nonpast) time (for example, *she walks*) and can take *-ing* to form the progressive (for example, *she is walking*).

adjective: By function, an adjective modifies a noun. By form, an adjective can have comparative and superlative forms, either by adding the suffixes *-er* and *-est* or the adverbs *more* and *most*.

Handout 13:2 Writing Dictionary Entries

For this exercise, you are going to create dictionary entries for words that you use but other people, maybe your parents or people from other places, might not understand. You will be writing definitions for two words that are different parts of speech. For each dictionary entry:

- Identify the part of speech by form.
- Write a definition echoing the tone of a standard dictionary.
- Compose a sentence illustrating the use of the word.

Follow your teacher's directions for other information about the exercise. Consider the example of *gully* as it is used below.

> I'd be lying if I said I knew where the verse from "Running Your Mouth" is from, but it is kinda **gully**. (Crawford, *XXL Magazine*)

In this context, it means to be strong, tough, or real. To figure out the part of speech, we can apply our tests. (Note that nouns don't need to pass all the tests. Some may pass only one of the three.)

Noun: Function Test	Noun: Form Test
can be the subject of a verb (a *book* sits . . . , the *swag* is . . .)	can be preceded by an article—*a/an/the* (a *book*, the *swag*)
	regular nouns can accept the plural marker -*s* in Standard English (*books*); note that irregular nouns can take different plural markers (*children, data, cacti*) and some nouns can't be counted (*swag, courage, progress, Miami*)
	can accept the possessive marker -*'s* in Standard English (the *dude's* car)

Verb: Function Test	Verb: Form Test
can accept a subject; a subject pronoun (*I, you, he, she, it, they*) can work for this test (I *sing*, they *study*)	can be marked for time—like past time, for example—either by changing form or being marked with the ending -*ed* in Standard English (*sang, studied*)
	can accept the third person singular marker -*s* for present time in Standard English (he *sings*, she *studies*)
	Can accept -*ing* to form the progressive (he is *singing*, she is *studying*)

Adjective: Function Test	Adjective: Form Test
modifies a noun (the *crazy* idea)	can have comparative and superlative forms, either by adding the suffixes -*er* and -*est* or the adverbs *more* and *most* (*crazier, most radical*)

We can use the form tests to figure out if *gully* is a noun. Can *gully* take an article? Or accept the plural and become *gullies*? A *gully* that is a kind of ditch can.

> In the water-cut **gullies** the earth dusted down in dry little streams. (*The Grapes of Wrath* by John Steinbeck)

Our use of *gully*, however, can't. We wouldn't say "a gully" or "gullies" in this sense. Perhaps it's a verb, then. Can it be marked for time? Would a construction like "Yesterday, he gullied" be possible? Again, the answer is no. Is it, finally, an adjective? Here is another example:

> Dre tries to prove he's "**gully**." (WH, *Time Out/London*)

In this sentence, *gully* is modifying *he*; it tells us what kind of person Dre is trying to prove he is. It is functioning as a adjective. But is it an adjective by form? Can someone be *gullier* than someone else? Or be *gulliest*? Here's an example from the same article as the first one:

> Then there's also the two "new" bonus tracks: a version of the original, **gullier** "One More Chance."

Gully, therefore, is without a doubt an adjective. So a dictionary entry might look something like:

> gully *adj.* 1. strong, tough 2. authentic, street <*He acts like he's gully but he's just a poser.*>

Handout 13:3 # Some Examples of Adjectival Suffixes

As has been noted, words that normally function as other parts of speech (like nouns) can sometimes function as adjectives. At other times, however, an adjective can be formed by adding a suffix to a word stem. Below is a partial list of adjectival suffixes. One of the most productive suffixes on the list is one of the simplest, *-y*. It is also interesting to note that these suffixes do not always follow our expectations. Why, for example, is *awful* an antonym and not a synonym for *awesome*?

Ending	Usage	Example
-able/-ible	capable of, tending to, likely to	. . . that turns even the most **respectable** men into scoundrels. (*Pirates of the Caribbean*)
-al	relating to, having the nature of	Geathers' hit on Green wasn't dirty or **intentional**. (Whitlock, ESPN)
-ant/-ent	doing a particular action, in a particular condition	Ricky Bobby is at once a creature of pure, **extravagant** absurdity. (Scott, *The New York Times*)
-er	comparative ending	Reality TV just gets **weirder** and **weirder**—and further from reality. (Hammond, *Cape Cod Times*)
-est	superlative ending	There was only the **slightest** smell of singed fur. (Morrison, *The Bluest Eye*)
-ful	full of, characterized by	. . . was chosen by "Idol" judges . . . out of thousands of **hopeful** contestants across the United States. (Taylor, *Spartan Daily*)
-ic	pertaining to, resembling	. . . the sudden **dramatic** events which make history. (Hansberry, *A Raisin in the Sun*)
-ish	having the qualities of	. . . and her face looked like the mask of an **impish** elf. (Angelou, *I Know Why the Caged Bird Sings*)
-ive	having a tendency to or the nature of	. . . a very special, very **expensive**, very large birthday present. (*The Little Mermaid*)
-less	without the qualities of, lacking	. . . Jen G. was lookin' rather plain-Jane in a **shapeless** black frock. (Casablanca, E! Online)
-like	having the qualities of	It was in this **godlike** state that he met Pauline Williams. (Morrison, *The Bluest Eye*)
-ose	full of, like	Sitting through all the **verbose** explanations and speculations about symbols, codes, secret cults . . . (McCarthy, *Variety*)
-ous/-ious	full of, having the qualities of	. . . on a glamorous trip way up North to the **fabulous** St. Louis. (Angelou, *I Know Why the Caged Bird Sings*)
-some	characterized by a quality or action	. . . those great and **awesome** wonders you saw with your own eyes. (Deuteronomy 10:21)
-y	having a quality of	Spitting his wry and wise rhymes over **Prince-y** synth beats . . . (Graves, *The Stranger Weekly*)

Objectives

- Students will practice identifying parts of speech.
- Students will practice their editing and revision skills.

Procedures

1. The purpose of this lesson is to have students review, edit, and finalize their dictionary entries. You might anonymously write one of each student's entries on the board or on an overhead. As a class, discuss them. Are the parts of speech correctly identified? Would everyone agree on the definitions? Are they stated clearly? Are the sample sentences descriptive and evocative? The other entry students can edit either individually or in small groups.

2. Have students type up their entries. The amount of class time you want to devote to typing the entries is up to you.

MATERIALS

Drafts of the students' dictionary entries

OTHER IDEAS

If you are interested in doing more with students' dictionary entries, you can have them edit, compile, and publish their entries either online or in print.

There are all kinds of activities that can be done with dictionaries. For example, students can "adopt" words of their own choosing or from classroom readings and be responsible for providing the class with background on their words including definitions and histories. Students can research word histories, which can be interesting and surprising. For example, a currently trendy word *swag* (meaning free stuff that is given away at a promotional event) takes on the meaning of *plunder*, a connotation very close to present-day usage, as early as 1794. Who knew? And if one can be *overwhelmed* and *underwhelmed*, can one simply be *whelmed*? (In fact you can. *Overwhelm* and *whelm* actually have similar meanings. Thus, *whelm* gets dropped from use and from *overwhelm* comes *underwhelm*.)

Verb Tense and Aspect and Subject-Verb Agreement

"Like systems for pronouns, systems for verbs have changed over time and vary across dialects."

Key Points

- Verb systems in English have changed over time and vary across dialects.

- Verb tense can be marked by changing endings or changing forms; aspect is often indicated by adding auxiliaries or modals to a main verb.

- In some Vernacular varieties, invariant *be* indicates a habitual action.

- In some Vernacular varieties, the third-person singular of regular verbs in the present tense is not marked. (There is no *-s*.)

- Distinguishing between dialect features and subject-verb agreement mistakes in students' writing is not always easy. Teachers need to pay attention to patterns of usage and rely on their knowledge of students and their language.

Background for Teachers

As I noted in the introduction to Lesson 5, verb tense locates an action in time and verb aspect indicates the perception of an action by a speaker (like whether that action is complete or habitual). Tense can be marked by adding suffixes like *-ed* to mark past time (in the case of regular verbs) or changing forms (in the case of irregular verbs like *to be* or *to sing*). Aspect is frequently indicated by the addition of auxiliaries or modals (like *be, do, have, can, would, should,* and so on) to a main verb.

Like systems for pronouns, systems for verbs have changed over time and vary across dialects. A change over time that is probably familiar to us is the use of *-th* instead of *-s* in marking the present tense third-person singular. We see this ending in Shakespeare:

> O, how this spring of love **resembleth**
> The uncertain glory of an April day

And we see it in the King James Bible:

> . . . and when he **seeth** thee, he will be glad in his heart.

Similarly, verb systems can vary across dialects. For example, some dialects do not use a suffix to mark the present tense third-person singular. Some of the characters in *A Raisin in the Sun* use this unmarked ending.

> Walter Lee **say** colored people ain't never going to start getting ahead.

We had a glimpse of how verb systems can vary when we looked at *ain't*. Such variation can get quite complex. We, of course, can only examine a small part of that complexity. The particular features we are going to look at are (1) habitual *be* and (2) third-person singular verbs that aren't marked with *–s*. I chose habitual *be* because it is a feature of a Vernacular variety that really stands out when people hear it, and I chose the third-person singular because it and similar features are likely to show up in students' writing.

Like its name suggests, habitual *be* designates an action that is customary or regularly repeated. In August Wilson's *Fences*, Bono asks

> How you figure he **be** making out with that gal **be** up at Taylor's all the time.

The verbs imply that his (Brownie's) efforts with the woman (Alberta) are customary and that Alberta is regularly at the Taylor's—and Wilson emphasizes the verbs with the adverbial "all the time." Used in this way, the verb *be* does not imply that either of these actions are going on right now, in the present moment.

It may be tricky for some students to recognize the difference between habitual *be* and infinitive *to be*. Habitual *be* takes the form of subject + *be* and is, then, distinct from uses like:

> She used **to be** real little. (Wilson, *The Piano Lesson*)

or

> Mr. Younger **would** just **be** plain mad if he could hear you talking foolish like that. (Hansberry, *A Raisin in the Sun*)

The other feature we are looking at—the third-person singular ending—is one that researchers have suggested tends to crop up frequently in students' writing. In Standard English, most verbs in the third-person singular present tense end with *-s*. In some Vernacular varieties, this ending has been dropped, so the third person is not marked.

> Dat's 'cause Tony **love** her too good. (Hurston, *Their Eyes Were Watching God*)

Throughout its history, English has shed many such endings like *-en* marking an infinitive.

> And palmeres for **to seken** straunge strondes. (Chaucer, *The Canterbury Tales*)

It has similarly lost *-en* marking present tense plurals.

ONLINE RESOURCES

Definition of Habitual Be

www.pbs.org/speak/about/guide/index.html#Habitual_be

Habitual Be Exercise

www.pbs.org/speak/education/training/seminar/sessiontwo.html#post_activities

Subject-Verb Agreement

www.csulb.edu/~wrl/handouts/SubjectVerbAgreement.pdf

And smale fowles **maken** melodye. (Chaucer, *The Canterbury Tales*)

And it has lost *-est* marking the present tense second-person singular.

Thou **woldest** been a trede-foul a-right. (Chaucer, *The Canterbury Tales*)

Given the number of changes over time, perhaps it isn't surprising that word endings of all kinds—those that mark tense or person for verbs, or possession for nouns—appear to be the writing features most influenced by dialect.

lesson plan **15** Verb Tenses

Objectives

- Students will become familiar with some of the basic properties of verbs like tense.
- Students will practice identifying various verb tenses.

Procedures

1. You might begin with a quick discussion/review of verbs. Some of the basic principles that might be worth touching on include the following.
   - Verbs are often described as "action words," but verbs can also describe processes that may not seem like actions, such as mental activities or states of being (*to be* is one of the most useful verbs in English).
   - By function, verbs can accept a subject. In the imperative (*Run!*), verbs don't have a subject, but verbs can accept a subject. A Standard English subject pronoun (*I, we, you, he, she, it, they*) makes a handy dummy subject (*I run*).
   - By form, verbs can be marked for time (like past time, for example, by adding *-ed* for regular verbs in Standard English). Also, in Standard English, verbs can accept the third-person singular marker *-s* in present (nonpast) time.
   - Verbs can be more that one word; they can be phrases.
2. If students have difficulty engaging in the discussion, it might help them to think back on their work with *ain't*. Think of the different ways *ain't* can function: *ain't much good, ain't running, ain't even started, ain't been sleepin'*. In each of these examples, the verbs are different and indicate a different timing for the action. As you review some basic properties of verbs, again, it isn't necessary for students to memorize the more technical names, like "present perfect progressive."
3. Distribute Handout 15:1.
4. Review the directions with students. Then have students complete the handout either individually or in small groups.
5. Review students' answers.

MATERIALS

Copies of Handout 15:1

OTHER IDEAS

Students may have some difficulty distinguishing between an event that happened in the past and one that happened in the past before another past action (that is, between past and past perfect), particularly if the quotations don't have any context. If this happens, you might have students imagine the context by inventing extensions to the quotations. This might help them puzzle out the verb tense/aspect that is being used.

Students might have some difficulty with example 3. In some Vernacular varieties, the construction *done* + main verb (V + *-ed/-en*) can have a variety of functions. The construction can indicate an action that has recently been completed (so the Standard equivalent would be roughly "I have just heard everything"), and the construction can also indicate what is called a resultant state, an emphasis on the state of the subject ("I have already heard everything"). This might be an interesting point to discuss.

ANSWER KEY

Handout 15.1

1. hadn't kidnapped, B
2. done heard, B
3. has been doing, A
4. 're gonna have to make, C

Handout 15:1 **Verb Tenses**

Verbs give readers or listeners a lot of information. Not only can they tell us the nature of an action or state (whether a person or thing is running or standing, stepping up or stepping off, going berserk or simply being), they can also tell us about the timing of an event, its relationship to other events, and a viewer's perception of that event. They can, for example, show that an action is continuing or hypothetical. Below are some short quotations. For each one, underline the verb, including auxiliary or "helping" verbs (for example, *will go*). Some are Standard and some are Vernacular. Remember that the verb can be more than one word; it can be a phrase. Then circle the letter of the response that most accurately completes the sentence.

1. From "Ballot or Bullet" by Malcolm X:

    . . . if some enemy hadn't kidnapped you . . .

    In the preceding quotation, the verb indicates an action that
    A. happened in the past (past)
    B. happened in the past before another past action (past perfect)
    C. is happening in the present (present)

2. Jay-Z in an MTV interview by Daniel Robert Epstein:

    Yeah, yeah. I done heard everything . . .

    In the preceding quotation, the verb indicates an action that
    A. happened in the past, continues in the present, and may continue in the future (present perfect progressive)
    B. happened in the past before another past action (past perfect)
    C. happened in the past (past)

3. From "What It Means to Be Colored in Capital of the U.S." by Mary Church Terrell:

    . . . it has been doing its level best ever since . . .

    In the preceding quotation, the verb indicates an action that
    A. happened in the past, continues in the present, and may continue in the future (present perfect progressive)
    B. happened in the past before another past action (past perfect)
    C. happened in the past (past)

4. George Clooney in the *Los Angeles Times* by Steven Smith:

    And we're gonna have to make it an ensemble!

    In the preceding quotation, the verb indicates an action that
    A. is happening in the present (present)
    B. happened in the past and is continuing in the present (present perfect)
    C. will happen in the future (future)

IMPORTANT TERMS

auxiliary verb: A verb that works in combination with a main verb. Together an auxiliary verb (or verbs) with the main verb form a verb phrase.

Auxiliary verbs are sometimes called *helping verbs*. Two of the most common auxiliary verbs in Standard English are *to be* and *to have*. Here are two important patterns using *be* and *have* (the auxiliary verb is bolded and the verb phrase is underlined):

1. *be* + main verb (V + *-ing*)

    She **is** <u>texting</u> her friend.

    We **were** <u>working</u> during class.

2. *have* + main verb (V + *-ed/-en*)

    He **has** <u>asked</u> his teacher.

    They **had** <u>taken</u> out their cell phones.

Other important auxiliary verbs include *to do, will, would, should, could, can, may,* and *might*. In some cases, you may find multiple auxiliary verbs (*she **will have been** <u>thinking</u> about*) or non-verbs in between the auxiliary the main verb (*they **had** courageously <u>tried</u>*).

lesson plan **16**   Uses of the Verb <u>to Be</u>

Objectives

- Students will practice identifying verb tenses/aspects.
- Students will identify some uses of the verb *to be*.

Procedures

1. You can begin by reminding students that they will be continuing their work on verb tense/aspect. You might ask them again, "What do verb tenses/aspects do?"

2. Next, you can tell them that they are going to look specifically at the verb *to be*. You might ask the students to conjugate the verb: In Standard English, what is *to be* in the present tense? First-person singular? Plural? Second? Third? (Note that some students may generalize *is*, as in *you is*. This is a systematic feature of some Vernacular varieties.) What about in the past tense? Then you might remind students that the verb *to be* has a variety of uses and those uses can vary in Standard and Vernacular English—they can think back to their work on *ain't*. In fact, it is, perhaps, because it is so useful and so common that *to be* is so irregular.

3. Distribute copies of Handout 16:1, and review the background information with students. I don't want to shy away from technical terms, but I don't want students or teachers to get hung up on the vocabulary. Depending on your own objectives and the level of your students, you can explore the vocabulary as much as you wish. However, students don't need the vocabulary to complete the lesson.

4. Distribute Handout 16:2.

5. If you do take a good deal of time reviewing the background on Handout 16:1, the activity itself can be kept short. As a class, discuss the scenario in Part I. Students may have other, social observations to make about the misunderstanding. This could be an interesting discussion, but you may also want to conserve time. If such a discussion begins to evolve, it is up to you to decide if it is worth pursuing.

6. Either as a class, in small groups, or individually, have students complete Part II. Students may have alternative responses. If they do, such responses are worth discussion. When discussion is complete, you can tell students that the use of *be* in this example is known as "habitual be."

MATERIALS

Copies of Handouts 16:1 and 16:2

OTHER IDEAS

It might be fitting while exploring the verb *to be* to discuss the passive voice. What is it? And how can we identify it? One particularly interesting question is "When can we use it?" The typical advice is to avoid it. It's true that overreliance on passive constructions can rob students' writing of energy. However, the passive voice is used extensively in the sciences; it shows up frequently in political speeches; and it can be a very useful tool. When would we use it and why?

ANSWER KEY

Handout 16:2

Part I

The disagreement arises because *be* as the student uses the verb is not equivalent to *is*.

Part II

1. B
2. A

The clue that these are the correct answers is the adverbial phrase *all the time*.

Handout 16:1 # Uses of the Verb <u>to Be</u>

BACKGROUND FOR STUDENTS

The ways in which verbs mark various forms has changed over time. A change that might be familiar is the use of *-th* instead of *-s* in marking the present tense third-person singular. We see this ending in Shakespeare:

> O, how this spring of love **resembleth** / The uncertain glory of an April day.

And we see it in the King James Bible:

> . . . and when he **seeth** thee, he will be glad in his heart . . .

Just as there are different verb systems at different times in history, there are different verb systems used by different groups of speakers. For example, some speakers do not use a suffix to mark the present tense third-person singular. Some of the characters in Lorraine Hansberry's *A Raisin in the Sun* use this unmarked ending.

> Walter Lee **say** colored people ain't never going to start getting ahead . . .

One verb that has many varied uses in both Standard and Vernacular systems is *to be*. The verb *to be* is one of the most common and useful verbs in the English language. By itself, it can be used to describe the qualities or state of something.

> I**'m** an actress, a brand, a businesswoman. I**'m** all kinds of stuff. (Associated Press, MSNBC)

When Paris Hilton says this, she is using the verb *to be* to make a claim about what and who she is.

In the previous lesson, we also saw how *to be* can also be used as an auxiliary verb in combination with a main verb. For example, when talking about his concert film, Jay-Z tells the interviewer:

> When I wasn't onstage, I **was changing** clothes. (Epstein, *Underground Online*)

The verb *was changing* is an example of the pattern *be* + main verb (V + *-ing*). Verbs that follow this pattern are sometimes called *progressive* or *continuous*.

Given that the verb *to be* has such a variety of uses, it's probably not surprising that Standard English and some Vernacular varieties of English sometimes use *to be* differently. In fact, we have already looked at two of those differences. We looked at *am not/is not/are not* versus *ain't*. And we looked at instances where a subject and an adjective are linked with the verb *to be* (*I am cognizant*) versus where it is implied (*you mad*).

Now we are going to look at another use of *to be*, one that probably sounds familiar to a lot of people but one that we may not think much about.

KEY POINTS

- *To be* is one of the most common verbs in the English language.
- Sometimes Vernacular varieties of English use *to be* differently than Standard English.
- *To be* can be a main verb, but it can also be an auxiliary verb.

Handout 16:2 **Uses of the Verb <u>to Be</u>**

Part I

The excerpt below was recorded in a Los Angeles elementary school (from *Talkin That Talk: Language, Culture and Education in African America* by Geneva Smitherman). Can you figure out and describe the cause of the miscommunication between the teacher and the student?

Teacher: Bobby, what does your mother do every day? (Teacher apparently wanted to call Bobby's parents.)
Bobby: She be at home!
Teacher: You mean, "She is at home."
Bobby: No, she ain't, 'cause she took my grandmother to the hospital this morning.
Teacher: You know what I meant. You are not supposed to say, "She be at home." You are to say, "She is at home."
Bobby: Why you trying to make me lie? She ain't at home.

Part II

Read the quotation below from August Wilson's *Fences* and answer the questions that follow.

How you figure he be making out with <u>that gal be</u> up at Taylor's all the time . . .

1. Choose the following phrase that you think would most accurately switch the underlined section of the quotation into Standard English.
    A. that gal who might be
    B. that gal who is usually
    C. that gal who had been
    D. that gal who used to be

2. The use of *be* in the preceding quotation describes an action that:
    A. is habitual or customary
    B. is hypothetical
    C. happened in the remote past
    D. happened in the past before another action

lesson plan 17 Code-Switching Using Habitual <u>Be</u>

MATERIALS

Copies of Handout 17:1

ANSWER KEY

Handout 17:1

Part I

In switching from the Vernacular habitual *be* to the Standard, students may have a variety of responses. Switching into Standard requires the addition of an adverb or adverbial phrase, so students may have answers that employ words like *usually, always*, and so on.

1. are usually
2. is always
3. be
4. am always

Rule X:

 . . . is indicated by *be*.

Rule Y:

 . . . is indicated by a form of *to be* plus *usually* or *always*.

Part II

Vernacular:

	SINGULAR	PLURAL
1st	be	be
2nd	be	be
3rd	be	be

Standard:

	SINGULAR	PLURAL
1st	am always	are always
2nd	are always	are always
3rd	is always	are always

Objectives

• Students will determine the grammatical rules governing the expression of habitual action in Standard and Vernacular English.

• Students will practice code-switching.

Procedures

1. You can remind students that they have been working with the verb *to be*. In particular, they have looked at one use of *to be* that indicates a habitual or customary action. Now, they will complete that work by explaining the grammatical rules that describe how people express habitual actions in Standard and Vernacular English.

2. Distribute Handout 17:1, and review the directions with students.

3. Have students complete the handout either individually or in small groups.

4. Review the students' responses. Note that habitual *be* is an invariant form. That is, it doesn't change by person or number. This is also true for some uses of *ain't*.

OTHER IDEAS

Time permitting, you might have a discussion with students about the social uses of habitual *be*. Who uses it? Do the students ever use it? Do they know people who use it? Is it ever used in writing? Why or why not? Do they ever hear it misused by speakers tying to imitate a Vernacular dialect?

Handout 17:1   # Code-Switching Using Habitual <u>Be</u>

For each of the following pairs, fill in the blank with the missing form. If the Vernacular form is given, provide the Standard equivalent, and if the Standard is given, provide the Vernacular. Then complete the rules that begin at the bottom and fill in the verb form chart for using *to be* to indicate a habitual action.

	System X = Vernacular	**System Y = Standard**
1.	But . . . <u>people be</u> lookin' for they little two minutes of fame. (Lil' Kim in *XXL* interview)	. . . people _____ looking . . .
2.	She never gives up, she always loves to train, pushing me around. <u>She be</u> tryin' to, but I don't let her get the upper hand. (Ron Coleman on WOWT)	. . . she _____ trying . . .
3.	. . . you _____ writing . . .	As a writer, <u>you're always</u> writing stuff from your life and things you remember of that. (Alan Jackson in CMT interview by Laura Douglas)
4.	<u>I be</u> right on top of everything, all the time. (Ronald "Slim" Williams in *Rolling Stone*)	I _____ right . . .
	Rule X: In some Vernacular varieties of English, a habitual action is indicated by:	**Rule Y:** In Standard English, a habitual action is indicated by:

Habitual action in some Vernaculars:

	Singular	**Plural**
First person (*I, we*)		
Second person (*you*)		
Third person (*he, she, it, they*)		

Habitual action in Standard English:

	Singular	**Plural**
First person (*I, we*)		
Second person (*you*)		
Third person (*he, she, it, they*)		

lesson plan 18 Code-Switching Using Third-Person Singular

MATERIALS

Copies of Handout 18:1

ANSWER KEY

Handout 18:2

1. says
2. keeps
3. play
4. tries
5. mean

Rule X:

. . . marked by nothing.

Rule Y:

. . . marked by s.

Objectives

- Students will practice conjugating verbs in the present tense.
- Students will practice code-switching.

Procedures

1. You might start by telling students that they will complete their work with verbs by looking at the differences in the endings of present tense verbs in Standard and Vernacular English.

2. Distribute copies of Handout 18:1.

3. Review the directions with students, and have them complete the handout either individually or in small groups.

4. Review students' responses. After the previous exercise with habitual *be*, this one should be fairly straightforward.

OTHER IDEAS

You might ask students how most Standard English verbs are conjugated in the present tense. Take an example from the handout *to say*:

First-person singular: *say*
Second-person singular: *say*
Third-person singular: *says*
First-person plural: *say*
Second-person plural: *say*
Third-person plural: *say*

All forms are consistent except for the third-person singular, which takes the ending -*s*. You might ask students if they can think of examples of Standard English verbs that don't follow this pattern. *To be* is one example. They might also come up examples of modals like *can*, *could*, *may*, *might*, *must*, *shall*, *should*, *will*, *would*. (These are special verbs; not only does the third-person singular not take an -*s*, but modals don't have an infinitive form—you can't say *to can* or *to may*.) They might also suggest *to do* or *to have*. These are interesting cases. *To do* actually follows the pattern (*he does*), but there is a pronunciation change (\d z\, not \duz\). *To have* is also close to the pattern with a slight difference. The third-person singular is *she has* not *she haves*. But try saying *haves*—it comes out sounding a lot like *has*.

Handout 18:1 # Code-Switching Using Third-Person Singular

For each of the following pairs, fill in the blank with the missing form. If the Vernacular form is given, provide the Standard equivalent, and if the Standard is given, provide the Vernacular. Then complete the rules that begin at the bottom.

	System X = Vernacular	System Y = Standard
1.	<u>The Bible say</u> an eye for an eye, a tooth for a tooth . . . (*The Piano Lesson* by August Wilson)	The Bible _____ an eye . . .
2.	<u>She keep</u> telling him no but be won't give up. (*A Raisin in the Sun* by Lorraine Hansberry)	She _____ telling him . . .
3.	. . . who _____ the piano . . .	And there's this other guy <u>who plays</u> the piano . . . (*A Raisin in the Sun* by Lorraine Hansberry)
4.	I see Berniece <u>still try</u> to be stuck up. (*The Piano Lesson* by August Wilson)	. . . Berniece still _____ to be . . .
5.	It _____ someone . . .	<u>It means</u> someone who is willing to give up his own culture . . . (*A Raisin in the Sun* by Lorraine Hansberry)
	Rule X: In some Vernacular varieties of English, a **third-person, present tense, verb** is usually marked by:	**Rule Y:** In Standard English, a **third-person, present tense, verb** is usually marked by:

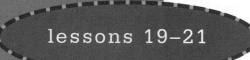

lessons 19–21

Code-Switching Review

Key Points

- Many different features can distinguish one dialect from another.
- The grammar of both Standard English and Vernacular varieties of English are systematic.
- Not all Vernacular features or disfluencies that appear in students' writing should be attributed to dialect.

Background for Teachers

So far, we have looked at the following grammatical features:

- the use of *ain't*
- implied *to be* before a predicative adjective
- reflexive pronouns
- habitual *be*
- unmarked third-person singular verbs in the present tense

There are, of course, other grammatical features that differentiate Standard and Vernacular Englishes. For example, two additional features that might arise in students' compositions are unmarked past tense (an absence of the -*ed* suffix) and unmarked possessives (an absence of -*'s*). Although it would take far too long to present every grammatical difference (entire books are dedicated to documenting the features of a single dialect), at this point, the hope is that by giving students and teachers a new way to think about language, as you come across features in readings or students' compositions, you will have some tools at your disposal for identifying and working with those features.[6]

My emphasis has been on the logic and systematicity of language, be it Standard or Vernacular. This emphasis should help make clearer to those students who use a variety of Vernacular English both the logic of their own language and the logic of the language that they are being asked to use in school. Similarly, it should help teachers to guide students in the process of switching between grammatical systems.

Teachers, of course, need to be prudent in their application of this approach. For example, a teacher might want to respond to an unmarked third-person singular verb in a student's composition. This may be an instance in which the teacher might want to prompt the student to code-switch. However, it might also be a simple typo or mistake—the kind that novice writers are prone to make. The teacher's decision on how to respond to and guide the student's writing will be influenced by the teacher's knowledge of the student's language use, a recognition of language use patterns, and an understanding of the student's rhetorical purpose.

In order to help students and teachers alike recognize patterns of linguistic features, the next two lessons will review the features we have studied thus far and also ask students to apply the techniques they've learned to some features we haven't studied. The lessons that follow these will move from the subject of code-switching and address some of the specific grammatical features of academic language.

ONLINE RESOURCES

American Varieties

www.pbs.org/speak/seatosea/americanvarieties/

AAE Grammar

www.stanford.edu/~rickford/ebonics/EbonicsExamples.html

Dialect Map of American English

www.uta.fi/FAST/US1/REF/dial-map.html

lesson plan 19 Code-Switching Review

MATERIALS

Copies of Handout 19:1

ANSWER KEY

Handout 19:1

1. C
2. A
3. C
4. B
5. A
6. B
7. B and C
8. B

   Note that *to be* in this example is in the infinitive; it is not habitual. If it were habitual, it might read something like, "I see Berniece still be stuck up."
9. C
10. B

Objectives

- Students will review features of Standard and Vernacular English.
- Students will practice code-switching.

Procedures

1. You might begin by asking students to name the Vernacular/Standard grammatical features they've studied so far. They should be able to identify the following:
   - the use of *like*
   - the use of *ain't*
   - implied *to be* before a predicative adjective
   - reflexive pronouns
   - habitual *be*
   - unmarked third-person singular verbs in the present tense

   If they have difficulty, you might prompt them.
2. Distribute Handout 19:1.
3. Review the directions with students. Note that C is a somewhat expanded rule from their previous work. They have studied *to be* absence before predicative adjectives. However, *to be* can be absent in other constructions, such as before a predicative noun or in a present progressive verb pattern *am/is/are* + (V + *-ing*). The extension of the rule is not overly complicated, and I have provided examples in the directions. Nonetheless, you might want to point out this extension to the students as you review the directions.
4. Have students complete the handout either individually or in small groups.
5. Review students' answers.

Handout 19:1 **Code-Switching Review**

 help!

Below are ten quotations from *The Piano Lesson* by August Wilson. Each one contains at least one of the following features:

A. habitual *be*
B. unmarked third-person, present tense singular
C. absence of *to be*
    This can be before a predicative adjective (. . . *she just tired*), a predicative noun (*We just plain working folks*), or a verb in the present progressive (*I know what you thinking about*).

Identify the feature or features (at least one quotation has two) in the quotations.

_____ 1.   They nice and lean.

_____ 2.   I know you can carry two hundred pounds! You be lifting them cotton sacks!

_____ 3.   She real nice.

_____ 4.   That dime say you can't be bashful.

_____ 5.   Mostly they be lonely and looking for somebody to spend the night with them.

_____ 6.   Uncle Doaker tell me your mama got you playing that piano.

_____ 7.   Boy Willy say you staying . . .

_____ 8.   I see Berniece still try to be stuck up.

_____ 9.   He my friend.

_____ 10. Let her sleep until she get up.

We've worked with predicative adjectives. Now we're talking about predicative nouns. What does it mean for a part of speech to be "predicative"?

The **predicate** is the part of a sentence or clause that is controlled by the verb. In a simple sentence, it is the verb and anything after it. For example, the predicate is underlined in the following: *She is tired*. Adjectives like *tired* can appear after verbs like *be*, *seems*, *appears*, and so on, as in the example. In these cases, they are in "predicative" position. Adjectives can also appear in front of nouns: *the tired athlete*, *the fierce ninja*, and so on. In this position, they are called **attributive**.

An adjective isn't the only part of speech that can be predicative. A noun can also follow the verb *to be*: *she is an athlete*, *he is a ninja*, and so on. There are, then, both predicative adjectives and predicative nouns. And some speakers do not use the verb *to be* to connect the subject of the verb and the predicative noun or adjective: *he a ninja*, *she tired*, and so on. Some speakers also do not use the verb *to be* in the Standard English pattern: *be* + main verb (V + *-ing*). Remember this verb pattern? It's sometimes called **progressive** or **continuous**. In the **present progressive**, *be* is in present time (*am/is/are*) in Standard English: *She is texting her friend*. In some Vernacular varieties, the auxiliary verb *am/is/are* is implied: *She texting her friend*.

lesson plan 20   Code-Switching Review, Continued

MATERIALS

Copies of Handout 20:1

OTHER IDEAS

If these kinds of features are showing up in your students' compositions, this exercise can have increased impact if you use writing samples from your own classroom.

ANSWER KEY

Handout 20:1

1. B
. . . the problem gets settled . . .
2. A
The character is frequently (or usually, often, and so on) in a situation . . .
3. B
. . . that tells you . . .
4. C
She is crying out . . .

Objectives

- Students will review features of Standard and Vernacular English.
- Students will practice code-switching.

Procedures

1. Remind students that they will be continuing their code-switching review.
2. Distribute copies of Handout 20:1.
3. Review the directions. Emphasize the note that precedes the directions. It reminds students that this is to be an exercise in code-switching, *not* error correction.
4. Have students complete the handout either individually or in small groups.
5. Review students' answers.

Handout 20:1 # Code-Switching Review, Continued

Note: In the following exercise, we are not practicing error correction. The examples below are perfectly grammatical expressions in Vernacular English. We want to practice code-switching into Standard English because, often, Standard English is the expectation in academic writing. This doesn't mean, however, that writing in Vernacular English can't be an effective and power-ful choice sometimes, as the earlier quotations by August Wilson attest.

Below are four quotations from sample essays. Each one contains at least one of the follow-ing features:

A. habitual *be*
B. unmarked third-person, present tense singular
C. absence of *to be*
   This can be before a predicative adjective (. . . *she just <u>tired</u>*), a predicative noun (*We just plain working <u>folks</u>*), or a verb in the present progressive (*I know what you thinking <u>about</u>*).

First, identify the feature or features in the quotations. Second, code-switch each of the quota-tions into Standard English.

_____ 1. Until the problem get settled, I think that the U.S. should be helping out the people who lost their houses.

_____ 2. The character be in a situation that he was not doing what he was supposed to.

_____ 3. If the poem is called "To an Athlete Dying Young," that tell you that the poem is going to be about life and death.

_____ 4. She crying out, trying to save her children.

lesson plan 21   Code-Switching Review, Continued

MATERIALS

Copies of Handout 21:1

Objectives

- Students will review features of Standard and Vernacular English.
- Students will practice code-switching.

Procedures

1. You can begin by telling students that after completing these activities on code-switching, their next set of lessons will address some of the specific grammatical features of academic English.

2. Distribute copies of Handout 21:1, and review the directions with students. You might emphasize that while we have looked at a few Vernacular features, grammatical systems, whether Standard or Vernacular, are quite complex. However, students should be able to apply the approaches they've been practicing to any grammatical feature that they come across.

3. Have students complete the handout individually.

4. Review their answers to the first part.

5. For the first two features, because we haven't studied them, you might ask students some questions. For example, what parts of speech are the examples? The *been* in the first sentence might be very interesting to discuss. What is the verb *been* indicating about the action in the first sentence? How does it locate the action in time? Its tense/aspect is somewhat ambiguous, but students might have some intuitions about it. It could be identified as a past tense form. It is likely to be code-switched into a present perfect verb (*have been*), indicating an action that happened at an indefinite time in the past and continues into the present. Others, however, have argued that this indicates a habitual action, like habitual *be*. Students may well argue for either interpretation.

6. Review students answers to the second part. You might do this by having them compare answers with a partner, having volunteers write their code-switched paragraphs on the board, or simply having volunteers read their responses aloud.

7. When you are done, it might be interesting to ask students, "Why didn't August Wilson simply write the dialogue in this standard form to begin with? What does he gain by using Vernacular English?"

ANSWER KEY

Handout 21:1

Below are the features that students might identify:

> They <u>been</u>[1] around here three days trying to sell <u>them</u>[2] watermelons. They <u>trying</u>[3] to get out to where the white folks live but the truck <u>keep</u>[4] breaking down. They go a block or two and it <u>break</u>[5] down again. They <u>trying</u>[6] to get out to Squirrel Hill and get around the corner. He <u>say</u>[7] <u>soon as</u>[8] he can get that truck empty to where he can set the piano up in there he <u>gonna</u>[9] take it out of here and go sell it.

1. a past tense form of *to be*, which would probably be a present perfect verb in Standard English
2. pronoun
3. implied *to be* before a progressive verb
4. unmarked third-person singular
5. unmarked third-person singular
6. implied *to be* before a progressive verb
7. unmarked third-person singular
8. subordinating conjunction
9. implied *to be* before a progressive verb indicating the future

Their paragraphs might look something like:

> They <u>have been</u> around here three days trying to sell <u>those</u> watermelons. They <u>are trying</u> to get out to where the white folks live but the truck <u>keeps</u> breaking down. They go a block or two and it <u>breaks</u> down again. They <u>are trying</u> to get out to Squirrel Hill and get around the corner. He <u>says</u> <u>as soon as</u> he can get that truck empty to where he can set the piano up in there he <u>will</u> [*or* <u>is going to</u>] take it out of here and go sell it.

Handout 21:1 **Code-Switching Review, Continued**

The following is a passage from the *Piano Lesson* by August Wilson (1990). First, circle any Vernacular grammatical features that you find. (**Note:** While we have studied most of the features that are present in this passage, there are at least a couple that we haven't.) After identifying the features, code-switch the passage into Standard English in the space below. When you are done, consider the result. Do you think the code-switched passage is more or less effective than the original? Why?

> They been around here three days trying to sell them watermelons. They trying to get out to where the white folks live but the truck keep breaking down. They go a block or two and it break down again. They trying to get out to Squirrel Hill and get around the corner. He say soon as he can get that truck empty to where he can set the piano up in there he gonna take it out of here and go sell it.

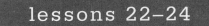

Topic/Comment Organization in Sentences

Key Points

- In writing, the basic building blocks of meaning are sentences and clauses.
- The communicative purpose of a piece of writing will strongly influence the expectations for the structure and organization of its sentences.
- The departure point of a sentence, its beginning, is called the topic.
- The destination of a sentence, its ending, is called the comment.
- Appropriate choices of sentence topics and comments will reflect the writing's purpose and will make a piece of writing seem coherent, organized, and complete.
- Inappropriate choices of topics and comments may make a piece of writing seem like it "doesn't flow," "lacks argument," "lacks focus," or is "undeveloped."

Background for Teachers

In our work thus far, we have been looking at how language varies across dialects. Our emphasis has been on systematicity—the ways in which dialects may have different verb tenses, pronouns, and so on, but those differences are logical and systematic. The features that we chose to illustrate contrasting systems have been word-level features (contrastive words like *himself*/*hisself* rather than, say, how interrogatives are constructed). Now we are going to change our focus in two ways.

First, we will be examining a different kind of variation. Rather than looking at variation *across* dialects, we will be looking at variation *within* a dialect. One example of this kind of variation would be relative formality. Standard English, for instance, can be used for very formal purposes like academic writing, but it can also be used for less formal purposes—writing emails, talking about sports, hanging out with friends. The same holds true for Vernacular dialects. They may

"Academic texts have a recognizable register— they tend to have features and structures that are preferred over other ones. Although these features are likely not transparent to students and teachers, we almost always respond to them, either positively or negatively."

be used for preaching in church, writing fiction (as we have seen), or talking with friends, and so on—a whole variety of purposes and a whole range of formality

As I mentioned in the book's Introduction (where I provided a definition), this type of variation is called *register*. While dialect variation can be significantly described by contrasting grammatical systems, register variation can be significantly described by contrasting vocabularies and organizations. At the end of the Introduction, I provided an illustration of register variation with three texts about surfing. Like each of those examples, academic texts have a recognizable register—they tend to have features and structures that are preferred over other ones. Although these features are likely not transparent to students and teachers, we almost always respond to them, either positively or negatively. They are often related to observations we make about development, coherence, and voice. An important objective for these lessons is to give students some concrete strategies for improving their writing when, for example, a teacher comments that their argument "needs development."

The first step in building up these skills is helping students to recognize some of the ways that sentences work. One way to think about how meaning gets made in a sentence is to think of a sentence, like a journey, as having two parts: a point of departure and a destination. The point of departure is simply the beginning of the sentence. This may be the sentence subject, but we can also begin sentences in other ways, with an adverbial or a prepositional phrase, for example. What a writer chooses as a point of departure has a big impact on how sentences relate to one another and how information gets organized. At the other end of a sentence, its destination is where the writer takes that sentence— how the writer builds on or expands his or her message.

For these lessons, we will be calling the sentence's point of departure its **topic** and the sentence's destination its **comment**. Many linguists and educators refer to these as **theme** and **rheme**. I have chosen an alternative terminology because **rheme**, while a useful technical term, would quite literally be Greek to students, and **comment** is both accessible and evocative.[7]

Identifying the topic and comment of a sentence is, most of the time, fairly straightforward. In simple, declarative sentences, the topic is the part of the sentence up to the verb, and the comment is the rest of the sentence. Here are some examples from a student's paper on *Pride and Prejudice*.

Jane	is led to believe that Bingley is interested in marrying her and she finds herself equally attracted to him.

Topic   **Comment**

Jane's facade of contentment and the repression of her feelings	only leave her unhappy and tormented.
Topic	**Comment**

Caroline's assurances that Bingley was attracted to Georgiana	broke down Jane's conviction even further.
Topic	**Comment**

In the preceding examples, the topic corresponds to the sentence subject. Topics, however, can include other elements that perform logical or linking functions like adverbials or conjunctions.

However, he	eventually realizes that he cannot be truly happy following his mind instead of his heart
Topic	**Comment**

And sentences can begin in other ways as well. The next example begins with a prepositional phrase.

To Jane, his attitude of seeming indifferent	was not only socially acceptable, but also encouraged by his family for it made his intentions of not marrying obvious to Jane.
Topic	**Comment**

My final example begins with a subordinate clause. One way to analyze this clause (and the way we are beginning with students) is to see the subordinate clause as the topic.

When Bingley leaves for London and does not return,	Jane follows him in hopes of an explanation.
Topic	**Comment**

As you work through the lessons with students, it is important to note that precision in identifying topics and comments is not the objective. The purpose is to give students a basic tool to analyze the way meaning is being constructed in their compositions. Some sentences can be messy and confusing. Deciding where the topic ends and the comment begins may not always be clear. That's okay and, in fact, can make for some interesting and productive discussions.

What is important for students to understand is that both the choice and organization of topic and comment are very important to their academic writing. What a writer chooses to put in topic position is made focal. So, for example, if a student were to write:

> I believe that Beloved represents Sethe's past experiences in slavery.

I would be in topic position, and the writer would be the focus rather than the character Beloved. This topic placement may not be particularly problematic in a single sentence, but if a pattern of topicalizing the writer were to emerge in a paper that was meant to focus on character analysis, the analysis would likely be perceived as weak (because the analysis would, quite literally, be grammatically backgrounded).

One potentially problematic pattern that commonly emerges in students' compositions is the repeated use of a character or literary feature like a symbol or motif as sentence topics. A student, for example, in writing about Hamlet's indecision, might repeatedly topicalize *Hamlet* or some variant like the pronoun *he*. (This pattern is evident in the second example of register variation below and in one of student paragraphs in Handout 22:1.) Of course, one can't avoid topicalizing the name of character when writing about literature. But what happens when a pattern of repetition lasts for the better part of a paragraph? For example, consider a series of sentences like these:

> Hamlet cannot decide to act. He is indecisive. For example, he says in his soliloquy, "To be or not to be." Hamlet is trying to make up his mind if he wants to live or die.

By identifying and placing the topics and comments into a T-graph, some problems become obvious.

Topic	Comment
Hamlet	cannot decide to act.
He	is indecisive.
For example, he	says in his soliloquy, "To be or not to be."
Hamlet	is trying to make up his mind if he wants to live or die.

First, the topic remains completely static. This is a common organization in encyclopedia entries, for example, but in a piece of analytical writing, this is problematic, in part, because static topics add incremental information about a single topic but don't develop any of the information in the comments. (We will be investigating this issue in detail in subsequent lessons.) Second, in literary analysis, abstract ideas often appear as topics. So here we might expect to see

---

IMPORTANT TERMS

topic: The beginning of a sentence or clause. Because of its initial position, it is both grammatically and thematically important.

comment: The part of the sentence or clause that follows the topic. It is the place where the writer develops the message of the sentence or clause, where the writer "comments on" the topic.

"Hamlet's inaction" as a topic somewhere. Third, the comments don't really go anywhere. The first two comments essentially repeat and the last, rather than interpreting the soliloquy, attributes another action to Hamlet.

In Lessons 22–24, we will be doing activities very similar to what we have done here with the paragraph on Hamlet. In Lesson 22, students will investigate register variation. In Lesson 23, they will practice identifying topics and comments. And in Lesson 24, they will work with a paragraph that has been separated into sentences, examine the topics and comments of those sentences, and then make some observations about topic/comment choice and how that influences the argument that paragraph is trying to make.

Finally, though we only work with some sample student texts in these lessons, having students repeat these activities with their own essays, either as a reflection or as a part of revision, can be extremely valuable in helping them to develop their fluency with academic language.

ONLINE RESOURCES

Theme/Rheme
www.tki.org.nz/r/esol/
esolonline/secondary_esol/
classroom/ncea/fat_tax/
task12_e.php

lesson plan **22** Language Variation According to Purpose

MATERIALS

Copies of Handout 22:1

OTHER IDEAS

You could add instructions for what you want students to identify in the passages: use of verbs (*to be*, passives, and so on), nouns and their modifiers, repetition, and so on.

ANSWER KEY

Handout 22:1

1. Students may find that C uses a lot more slang than A or B. They may say that C seems more action-oriented than A or B, which they may find to be more descriptive. A uses a lot of verbs related to thinking and saying; B uses a lot of the verb *to be*; and C uses a lot of active verbs.
2. Either A or B may be considered the most formal. Students most likely will argue that C is the least. They may observe that C uses a less formal vocabulary and uses incomplete sentences.
3. Answers for this question will vary, but A is from a newspaper article, B is from an encyclopedia, and C is from a blog.

Objectives

- Students will be introduced to the concept of register variation.
- Students will begin recognizing how language varies according to rhetorical purpose.

Procedures

1. You can begin by telling students that after completing these activities on code-switching, their next set of lessons will address some of the specific grammatical features of academic English.
2. Distribute copies of Handout 22:1, and review the directions with students. You might emphasize that while we have looked at a few Vernacular features, grammatical systems, whether Standard or Vernacular, are quite complex. However, students should be able to apply the approaches they've been practicing to any grammatical feature that they come across.
3. Have students complete the handout as a class, in small groups, or individually.
4. Review their answers.

Handout 22:1 # Language Variation According to Purpose

Up to now, we have been studying how language can vary depending on the person who is speaking. Now we are going to change our focus. We will be looking at how language can vary depending on our purpose for communicating.

    Following are three excerpts. All three are written in Standard English, and all three are written about surfing. However, they are all observably different. Read the excerpts, and then answer the questions that follow.

A. It is unclear why surfing has found a broader respectability. Some point to the initial public offering of Quiksilver, the board apparel and accessories company, in 1986 as a catalyst. Perhaps reflecting surfing's laid-back roots, concrete figures on participation are hard to come by. Two million people consider themselves active surfers in the United States, twice as many as 20 years ago, according to Action Sports Retailer, the leading board-sports industry trade show.

B. Modern surfboards are constructed of a plastic foam core that is shaped by hand or machine and then covered with a shell of fiberglass and resin. Individual surfboards can vary in dimensions. The high performance surfboards used by top professional competitors are typically about 1.8 to 2 m (6 to 6.5 ft) long, 47 cm (18.5 in) wide, less than 6 cm (2.5 in) thick, and weigh about 2.7 kg (6 lb). These boards are also known as shortboards. On the other end of the surfboard spectrum is the longboard. Most longboards are 2.7 m (9 ft) long, 51 to 56 cm (20 to 22 in) wide, and about the same thickness as shortboards. They weigh less than 7 kg (15 lb).

C. Wow . . . definitely a night and day scenario. Headed out to DH early yesterday morning for a quick surf on the Bing. Small kine waves rolling through with hardly a wisp of wind. Super fun to be loggin it again. Good chance for me to get back into shape before going back to the northshore. Managed to get one killer wave . . . it walled up about waist high for a nice long hang ten, then back stepped as it pitched a bit to get a teeny weeny coverup, more like water splashing on my shoulder, but felt good. Zipped through that section and the wave opened up again for a another noseride with a fade back. Good fun and all to myself!

Questions

1. Identify and describe three differences among the passages. Be as specific as you can. For example, do they use different vocabularies? Verbs?

2. Rank the three excerpts in order of formality from the most formal to the least, and give reasons for your ranking.

3. Where do you think each passage comes from? Why?

lesson plan 23   Introduction to Topic/Comment

MATERIALS

Copies of Handouts 23:1 and 23:2

ANSWER KEY

Handout 23:2

A. Topic 1 begins with something general (surfboards), and subsequent topics are more specific subclasses (high-performance surfboards, longboards, and so on).

B. Important purposes of encyclopedia entries are to identify and define. One way to serve those purposes is to talk about a thing and the parts that make up that thing (like the pupil and iris of an eyeball or the tail and fur of a squirrel). Another way is to talk about a class of things and different members of that class (red squirrels and gray squirrels or high-performance surfboards and longboards). The kinds of derived topics that you see in this example, then, serve the rhetorical purposes of encyclopedia entries very well.

Objectives

- Students will be introduced to the concept of topic/comment structure.
- Students will begin to examine the importance of topic/comment selection as a rhetorical strategy.

Procedures

1. You might begin by reminding students that they will shift their focus from examining code-switching to looking at some of the specific features of academic writing.

2. Distribute Handout 23:1.

3. Review the handout with students. These concepts are likely new and somewhat more technical than other exercises they have done. If they are concerned, emphasize that they will have opportunities to work with these concepts and, in some ways, they are more difficult to explain than to actually use.

4. Distribute Handout 23:2 and review the directions.

5. Discuss the questions as a class. Some classes may see the relationship very quickly. Others may need some prompting.

Handout 23:1 # Introduction to Topic/Comment

BACKGROUND FOR STUDENTS

How do sentences work? One way to think about the workings of a sentence is to compare it to a journey: It has a point of departure and moves to a destination. The point of departure is important because it orients us; it lets us know what we're focusing on. And, clearly, the destination is important, too. This, after all, is where we end up.

We're going to be calling a sentence's point of departure its **topic** and a sentence's destination its **comment**. The topic of a sentence is just the beginning of a sentence, and it is what the sentence is about. The comment is the rest of the sentence. It's what the writer has to say about the topic. Here are some examples from student papers on *Pride and Prejudice*.

1.

Jane	is led to believe that Bingley is interested in marrying her and she finds herself equally attracted to him.

Topic   **Comment**

2.

Jane's facade of contentment and the repression of her feelings	only leave her unhappy and tormented.

Topic   **Comment**

3.

Caroline's assurances that Bingley was attracted to Georgiana	broke down Jane's conviction even further.

Topic   **Comment**

4.

However, he	eventually realizes that he cannot be truly happy following his mind instead of his heart.

Topic   **Comment**

5.

To Jane, his attitude of seeming indifferent	was not only socially acceptable, but also encouraged by his family for it made his intentions of not marrying obvious to Jane.

Topic   **Comment**

6.

When Bingley leaves for London and does not return,	Jane follows him in hopes of an explanation.

Topic   **Comment**

KEY POINTS

- In writing, the basic building blocks of meaning are sentences and clauses.
- The communicative purpose of a piece of writing will strongly influence the expectations for the structure and organization of its sentences.
- Appropriate choices of sentence topics and comments will reflect the writing's purpose and will make a piece of writing seem coherent, organized, and complete.
- Inappropriate choices of topics and comments may make a piece of writing seem like it "doesn't flow," "lacks argument," "lacks focus," or is "undeveloped."

IMPORTANT TERMS

topic: The beginning of a sentence or clause. Because of its initial position, it is both grammatically and thematically important.

comment: The part of the sentence or clause that follows the topic. It is the place where the writer develops the message of the sentence or clause, where the writer "comments on" the topic.

You might notice that the comment, most of the time, starts at the verb (or the adverb modifying the verb). The exception here is 6. Sentence 6 is actually made up of two clauses, which just means there are two subjects (*Bingley* and *Jane*) and two verbs (*leaves* and *follows*). I've ended the topic at the end of the first clause.

You also might notice that some topics (like 1) are simple, and others (like 2 and 3) are complex.

In the following exercises, you will practice identifying topic and comments. Sometimes separating the topic and comment will be clear, sometimes (like in 6) it may not be. It's okay if you identify the topic slightly differently from someone else. What will be important as we move through these lessons is understanding that our choices of sentence topics and how we organize them have a big impact on the success of our academic writing.

Handout 23:2 # Introduction to Topic/Comment

Below is the excerpt from *Encarta* about surfboards. A T-graph has been made separating the topic and comment of each sentence. Using the information in the graph, answer the questions that follow.

	Topic	Comment
1.	Modern surfboards	are constructed of a plastic foam core that is shaped by hand or machine and then covered with a shell of fiberglass and resin.
2.	Individual surfboards	can vary in dimensions.
3.	The high performance surfboards used by top professional competitors	are typically about 1.8 to 2 m (6 to 6.5 ft) long, 47 cm (18.5 in) wide, less than 6 cm (2.5 in) thick, and weigh about 2.7 kg (6 lb).
4.	These boards	are also known as shortboards.
5.	On the other end of the surfboard spectrum	is the longboard.
6.	Most longboards	are 2.7 m (9 ft) long, 51 to 56 cm (20 to 22 in) wide, and about the same thickness as shortboards.
7.	They	weigh less than 7 kg (15 lb).

DISCUSSION QUESTIONS

A. How would you describe the relationship between the topics? For example, are they all more or less the same? Are they specific examples of a general class of thing?

B. For encyclopedia entries, this is a very common topical pattern. Why? How does this pattern serve the purpose of an encyclopedia?

If a topic is the beginning of a sentence or clause and a comment is the end of a sentence or clause, what is a sentence? And what is a clause? And how are they different?

A **clause** is a grammatical unit, a grouping of words, that has both a subject and a predicate. In other words, a clause has both a subject (a doer) and a verb (an action).

Some clauses can stand alone as sentences. These clauses are called **independent clauses**. Here is an example: *my surfboard broke*. The subject is *my surfboard* and the predicate is *broke*.

Some clauses cannot stand alone as sentences. These clauses are called **dependent clauses**. Here is an example: *because I hit the reef*. The subject is *I* and the predicate is *hit the reef*.

A **sentence** can have multiple clauses but it must have at least one independent clause: *Because I hit the reef, my surfboard broke.*

lesson plan 24 Topic/Comment in Academic Writing

MATERIALS

Copies of Handout 24:1

OTHER IDEAS

You can have students select paragraphs from their own writings and plot the topics and comments using T-graphs, underlining, or any convenient method. How would they evaluate their own choices? Are they mostly simple or complex? How would they characterize their topics? Do they have any abstract topics? Or are most of their topics people?

Objectives

- Students will know the definitions of topic and comment.
- Students will be able to identify topic and comment in sample sentences.

Procedures

1. You might begin by reminding students that they will be continuing to focus on some of the specific features of academic writing.

2. Distribute Handout 24:1.

3. Review the directions with students. If students have difficulty with the concept of topic/comment, you could compare the role of the topic in a sentence to a topic sentence in a paragraph. A topic sentence should orient the reader and frame the paragraph just as the topic of a sentence orients a sentence to what is to follow. Also, you might emphasize that separating the topic from comment is not always precise, and it's okay if their answers are not all exactly the same.

4. Have students complete the first part of the handout either individually or in small groups.

5. Review their responses.

6. As a class discuss questions A, B, and C at the bottom of the handout. The notion of simple versus complex topics need not be overly complicated. Are there many words or few? Is there a simple noun subject in the topic or other components? Question C can be particularly relevant to students' academic writing.

ANSWER KEY

Handout 24:1

1. <u>Shakespeare</u> pinpoints hesitation and overrationalization as the source of his ultimate ruin.
2. <u>Once again, Hamlet's unnecessary observation</u> keeps him from taking the life of Claudius.
3. <u>The combination of Hamlet's omnipresent logic and fear of action</u> cripple his attempts at revenge.
4. <u>He</u> believes that the spirit could be a devil "assum[ing] a pleasing shape . . . to damn [him]."
5. <u>Time and time again, Hamlet</u> waits for the ideal opportunity to avenge his father.
6. <u>Each occasion that presents itself</u> never reaches fruition because Hamlet's rationality outweighs his passion.

Discussion Questions

A. 1. simple; 2. complex; 3. complex; 4. simple; 5. complex or simple (depending on whether one sees the adverb phrase as moving the topic beyond simple); 6. complex.

B. 1. person; 2. other or perhaps event; 3. concept; 4. person; 5. person; 6. event.

C. Of course, **all of these** are important. What students may not be aware of is that topicalizing abstractions is a key component of academic writing. Narratives, for example, frequently topicalize people, but most academic writing features a good number of more abstract, nonpeople topics.

Handout 24:1 # Topic/Comment in Academic Writing

The following sentences are from a student's essay on *Hamlet*. For each of the sentences below, underline the topic:

1. Shakespeare pinpoints hesitation and overrationalization as the source of his ultimate ruin.

2. Once again, Hamlet's unnecessary observation keeps him from taking the life of Claudius.

3. The combination of Hamlet's omnipresent logic and fear of action cripple his attempts at revenge.

4. He believes that the spirit could be a devil "assum[ing] a pleasing shape . . . to damn [him]."

5. Time and time again, Hamlet waits for the ideal opportunity to avenge his father.

6. Each occasion that presents itself never reaches fruition because Hamlet's rationality outweighs his passion.

Discussion Questions

A. For each of the sentences 1–6, characterize the topic as either simple or complex.
B. For each of the sentences 1–6, characterize the topic as one of the following: a person or character; a concept or idea; an event; something else (please specify).
C. What kinds of topics (people, concepts, events, or other) do you think are most important in the writing you do in your English class?

 **help!**

Where does the topic end and the comment begin?

Most of the time, the topic includes all of the words up to the verb phrase. A **verb phrase** includes all of the words (auxiliary verbs, adverbs, and so on) that work together with the main verb to provide information about the action—when it's taking place, how long, and so on. A verb phrase may include just one word, the main verb, or many. Here are two examples with the verb phrase underlined:

> I <u>know</u> . . .

> I'<u>m about to break</u> the rules . . .

For these examples, the topic ends at the verb phrase, so the topic would be *I*. If you can't reason out the break between topic and comment, use your intuitions. Most of the time, this break will seem very natural.

The Known/New Contract and Information Structure

Key Points

- There is a general preference in writing to have known information appear before new information.

- Fulfilling the known/new contract can be achieved using three basic topical patterns: constant, derived, and chained.

- Most writing tasks make use of all three patterns, but some tasks have a preferred one.

- Inappropriate use of or overreliance on a pattern can result in writing that is ineffective.

Background for Teachers

In the previous three lessons, I introduced the concept of topic/comment organization in sentences and began to discuss how the composition of topics and comments can affect the larger organization of a paragraph. Now I want to build upon those basic concepts in order to help students better understand how topic/comment structure influences the coherence and development of a paragraph and how to more effectively choose what they want to put in the topic position of any given sentence.

The concept that will be the focus of these next lessons is the known/new contract.[8] The essence of the known/new contract is a fairly simple idea: As readers, we prefer information that we know to come before information that is

> "The essence of the known/new contract is a fairly simple idea: As readers, we prefer information that we know to come before information that is new."

IMPORTANT TERMS

known/new contract: The preference for information that is known to come before information that new in a sentence or clause.

new. In conjunction with what we've learned in previous lessons, this means that it is most often preferable to have known information in the topic position and new information as comment.

Fulfilling the known/new contract can be accomplished using three basic methods: repetition of a previous topic (a constant pattern), derivation from a previous topic (a derived pattern), or adoption of a previous comment (a chained pattern).

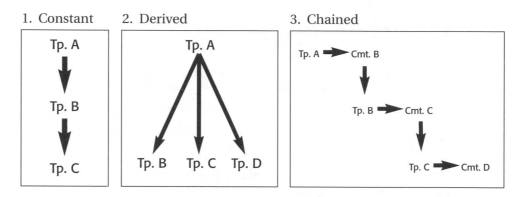

Repetition is probably the most obvious strategy (a constant pattern). Using repetition, the writer simply repeats (directly or using a form of substitution) some or all of a previous topic:

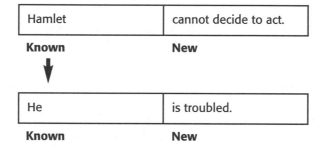

In the above example, known *Hamlet* becomes known *He*. Often the repeated topic will come from the sentence immediately before it, but it may come from even earlier in a sequence of sentences. (Although the farther the repeated topic is from the original, the greater the likelihood the repeated topic is to appear to the reader to be new rather than known information.)

A second method for placing known information in the topic is to derive a topic from a previous one. Such derivation requires that the initial topic be generalized in some way such that latter topics can be examples or characteristics of that first, root topic. This is a common organization in encyclopedias (a pattern that we saw in the surfboard entry).

All of the characters in the play	are flawed.
Known	**New**

↓

Hamlet, for example,	cannot decide to act.
Known	**New**

A third strategy for organizing information is to take up the comment of a previous sentence and restate it as the topic.

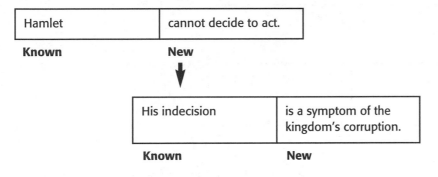

Hamlet	cannot decide to act.
Known	**New**

↓

His indecision	is a symptom of the kingdom's corruption.
Known	**New**

All three strategies are important to students' writing. However, we are going to concentrate here on helping students to develop this third strategy. Although the first two strategies of repetition and derivation are clearly useful ways of organizing information, and they should be pointed out to students, they are methods that are more intuitive and ones students have practiced (whether or not they are aware of it) while doing reports in elementary and middle school, for example.

The third method of taking up new information, topicalizing it, and generating additional new information is an organizational structure that students are probably not aware of and one that seriously affects their ability to develop arguments. Indeed, very often when teachers respond to a place in a student's essay with "needs development," the student has introduced some important new information but has failed to take it up in any subsequent sentence.

Let's take another look at an excerpt we introduced earlier when we were examining topic/comment structure.

> Hamlet cannot decide to act. He is indecisive. For example, he says in his soliloquy, "To be or not to be." Hamlet is trying to make up his mind if he wants to live or die.

Combining what we learned about topics and comments with our understanding of the known/new contract, we can say a little bit more about how and why this segment of text fails. Tracking the known/new information would look something like this.

Hamlet	cannot decide to act.
Known	**New**

↓

He	is indecisive.
Known	**New**

↓

For example, he	says in his soliloquy, "To be or not to be."
Known	**New**

↓

Hamlet	Is trying tomake up his mind if he wants to live or die.
Known	**New**

ONLINE RESOURCES

Achieving Coherence in Writing

www.boisestate.edu/
wcenter/ww97.htm

The Known-New Contract

www.d.umn.edu/
~dmorriso/readablewriting/
Coherence/known-new
%20contract.html

The first problem we might notice is that the second sentence doesn't actually introduce any new information. Another more global problem is that Hamlet's indecision is introduced as new information but is never taken up as a subsequent topic. Thus, what develops is less an analysis of Hamlet's inability to act and more of a description of Hamlet's actions, or lack thereof. This, in fact, is the very kind of writing that is likely to be met with a response of "needs development" or "too descriptive."

So how might a student revise a piece of writing like this? One strategy (though not the only one) might be something like this.

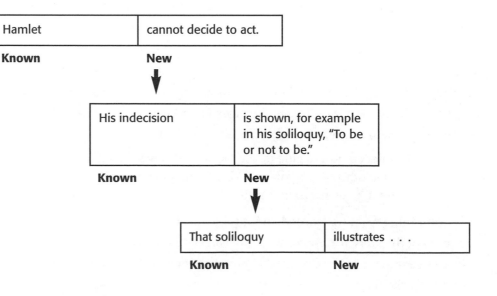

Hamlet	cannot decide to act.
Known	**New**

↓

His indecision	is shown, for example in his soliloquy, "To be or not to be."
Known	**New**

↓

That soliloquy	illustrates . . .
Known	**New**

I don't want to suggest here that sentences should always and forever progress in this way. Certainly, in an argument such as this one, the student is going to have organize information in a variety of ways. However, by making students aware of the known/new contract and the importance of topicalizing new information at critical moments in their writing, their writing can improve dramatically.

We will be workng with students' writing on *Beloved* and *All the Pretty Horses* as we familiarize students with the concept of known/new organization. Then, students will practice both predicting and composing sentence topics.

lesson plan **25**   **The Known/New Contract**

MATERIALS

Copies of Handout 25:1 and 25:2

ANSWER KEY

Handout 25:2

1. A (constant)
2. C (chained)
3. B (derived)
4. D (none)

Objectives

- Students will be introduced to the known/new contract.
- Students will begin identifying some basic topical patterns.

Procedures

1. You could start the lesson by telling students that they will continue to look at how sentences work. In particular, they will look at how sentences fit together and how they can address issues like "lack of development" in their essays.

2. Distribute Handout 25:1.

3. Review the information with students. You might emphasize that while the known/new contract is very important to understand, it is not unbreakable. There are times when writers can effectively choose to place new information first—for example, to foreground an important point. The known/new contract should guide their composing, not inhibit it. If you use curriculum that prescribes certain paragraph structures or the rhetorical function of particular sentences within a paragraph (for example, that the first sentence is a topic sentence, that the second sentence introduces some kind of evidence, that the third sentence analyzes that evidence, and so on), introducing students to the ways in which information connects sentences can strengthen their paragraphs based on such boilerplates. Students can begin to see how sentences can fulfill a particular rhetorical purpose but also grammatically dovetail with surrounding sentences.

4. Distribute Handout 25:2

5. Have students complete the handout either as a class, individually, or in small groups.

6. Review their responses.

Handout 25:1   # The Known/New Contract

BACKGROUND FOR STUDENTS

In the previous exercises, we worked with topics and comments and began to think about how they are arranged and how we can organize our sentences to make our writing more effective. We are now going to explore some organizational strategies in more detail.

In particular, we are going to work with the known/new contract. The known/new contract has to do with the organization of information. It simply states that in writing, we prefer to have information that we know come before information that we don't. In other words, it is better, most of the time, to have known information in the topic and new information in the comment.

Fulfilling the known/new contract can be accomplished using three basic methods: repetition of a previous topic (a constant pattern), derivation from a previous topic (a derived pattern), or adoption of a previous comment (a chained pattern).

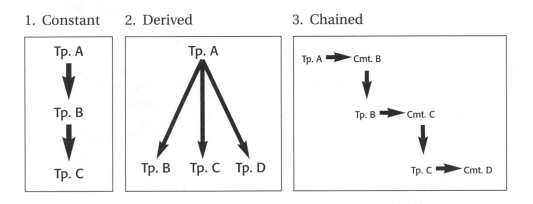

Repetition is probably the easiest strategy (a constant pattern). Using repetition, you simply repeat (directly or using a form of substitution) some or all of a previous topic.

Hamlet	cannot decide to act.
Known	**New**

↓

He	is troubled.
Known	**New**

A second method for placing known information in the topic is to derive a topic from a previous one. We saw the derived pattern earlier in the encyclopedia entry about surfboards. In this pattern, the first topic is the whole (like a squirrel) or a general class of things (like surfboards), and the subsequent topics are parts (like the tail, the eyes, and so on) or specific examples (like high-performance surfboards, longboards, and so on).

All of the characters in the play	are flawed.
Known	**New**

↓

Hamlet, for example,	cannot decide to act.
Known	**New**

Probably the most difficult and most important pattern to master is the chained pattern. To use this strategy, you take up the comment of previous sentence and restate it as the topic.

Hamlet	cannot decide to act.
Known	**New**

↓

His indecision	is a symptom of the kingdom's corruption.
Known	**New**

From these two examples, we can see that information can progress from topic to topic or from comment to topic.

But what happens when the known/new contract is violated? Sometimes, it's okay. Maybe we want to emphasize a key point, so we'll put new information in the topic. Usually, however, when the contract is violated, the clarity of our writing suffers.

The kingdom of Denmark	is being slowly corrupted.
Known	**New**

Claudius' influence	only makes Hamlet delay even more.
New	**New**

Although these two sentences may seem related somehow, the second doesn't seem to follow from the first because neither the idea of the kingdom nor its corruption is taken up.

Identifying what is known and what is new can be tricky. Sometimes a topic may take up some known information but also add to it and introduce a little new information, too. That's okay. As readers, as long as there's a kernel of known information and not too much new information in a topic, we can follow along.

KEY POINTS

- There is a general preference in writing to have known information appear before new information.
- Fulfilling the known/new contract can be achieved using three basic topical patterns: constant, derived, and chained.
- Most writing tasks make use of all three patterns, but some tasks have a preferred one.
- Inappropriate use of or overreliance on a pattern can result in writing that is ineffective.

IMPORTANT TERMS

known/new contract: The preference for information that is known to come before information that new in a sentence or clause.

In cases where there's a mix of known and new, we might not all agree on what to call a particular topic or comment. What is important for our writing is recognizing the importance of adhering to the known/new contract most of time.

There are also topics that can be confusing because they don't contain any information at all.

It	is impossible to act when consumed by doubt.
Topic	**Comment**

There	is not enough time to let one's mis-takes dominate life.
Topic	**Comment**

In the preceding sentences, to what are the *It* and *There* referring? In short, nothing! These are empty topics that allow us to emphasize the new information in a comment. For the sake of consistency, we'll call these empty topics known information.

Handout 25:2 # Known/New Patterns

Each of the following examples are taken from students' essays analyzing *Beloved*. For each one, identify the topical pattern as:

A. Constant
B. Derived
C. Chained
D. None

None implies that there is no apparent connection topic to topic or comment to topic.

1. _____

Topic	Comment
Paul D	witnesses the burning of one best friend and the insanity of another.
He	also struggles with his own dehumanization and slavery in a chain gang.

2. _____

Topic	Comment
In the novel *Beloved,* Toni Morrison	creates a poignant and compelling story about Sethe, a strong ex-slave living with her daughter and struggling to overcome her past.
Sethe's tragic and disturbing past	refuses to be ignored.

3. _____

Topic	Comment
Characters in the novel *Beloved*	fight against their memories of slavery.
Sethe, for example,	refuses to face her past memories by "remembering the wonderful soughing trees rather than the boys" who cruelly took advantage of her.

4. _____

Topic	Comment
In *Beloved,* trees	are an important symbol of the past.
The murder of one daughter and near killing of her other three children	are haunting incidents for Sethe.

lesson plan 26 Identifying Known/New Information

Objectives

- Students will apply the concept of the known/new contract.
- Students will begin identifying topics and comments as containing either known or new information.

Procedures

1. You could start the lesson by telling students that they will continue to look at known/new information. In particular, they will look at an example where the known/new contract is violated and how that impacts the effectiveness of the writing.

2. Distribute Handout 26:1 and review the directions.

3. Have students complete the first part of the handout either individually or in small groups.

4. Review their responses.

   Some potential issues to keep in mind:

   - It's okay to assume prior knowledge for the first topic (thus making it known). However, keep students focused on the context of the paragraph only for the rest of the sentences.
   - Sentence #3 is a possible hang-up. Here, the pronoun *It* is existential, having no referent. In this way, it is an empty topic that functions as known information.
   - Another place of ambiguity might be sentence #5. Here, the comment is clearly repeating that of sentence #2. However, they are separated enough that some students might not notice the repetition. It might be useful to discuss how far apart information can be before we no longer recognize it as known.

5. You might have students prepare responses to the discussion questions individually or in small groups and then compare answers as a class. Or you might simply engage the questions in whole-class discussion.

OTHER IDEAS

If you would like to reinforce the previous material, you could have student, identify the known/new patterns sentence to sentence in this paragraph.

MATERIALS

Copies of Handout 26:1

ANSWER KEY

Handout 26:1

1. K (or N), N
2. N, N
3. K (empty topic), N
4. K, N
5. K, K (from sentence #2)
6. K, N (or perhaps K if the comment is seen as repeating #2)

Discussion Questions

A. It is fairly clear that the information structure breaks down in the second sentence. Students may also note that sentence #5 could be viewed as repetitive, and sentence #6 is also possibly repetitive.

B. Students will have a variety of responses. One piece of advice students might offer is that the writer introduces some significant information in the first, topic sentence: blood represents power, courage, and pride. The second sentence, however, introduces new information about John's fantasy of being a cowboy. This latter information is what is built upon through subsequent topics and comments, and the symbolism of the blood is largely abandoned. Students might suggest that the writer either compose a different topic sentence or pursue the information that has been introduced in the current one.

Handout 26:1 # Identifying Known and New Information

Below is a paragraph from a student paper analyzing *All the Pretty Horses* by Cormac Mc-Carthy. The book describes the adventures of a Texas teenager, John, who rides into Mexico. The paragraph we will be looking is as follows:

> In *All the Pretty Horses,* blood is a sign of power, courage, and even pride. John's fantasy of becoming a cowboy stems from "what [John] loved in horses was what he loved in men, the blood and the heat of the blood that ran them." It is the fantasy of being a cowboy that keeps him alive. It is also a life of violence. He sees the horses as sharing his lifeblood. The horses embody his dream of being a true cowboy.

I have divided the paragraph into topics and comments. Before each topic and after each comment is a line. Identify each topic and each comment as either known or new information, and then write a *K* (known) or *N* (new) on the line.

	Topic	Comment	
1. ____	In *All The Pretty Horses*, blood	is a sign of power, courage, and even pride.	____
2. ____	John's fantasy of becoming a cowboy	stems from "what [John] loved in horses was what he loved in men, the blood and the heat of the blood that ran them."	____
3. ____	It	is the fantasy of being a cowboy that keeps him alive.	____
4. ____	It	is also a life of violence.	____
5. ____	He	sees the horses as sharing his lifeblood.	____
6. ____	The horses	embody his dream of being of a true cowboy.	____

Discussion Questions
A. Where in the paragraph does the known/new contract break down?
B. Applying your knowledge of the known/new contract, what would you recommend that the student do to improve this paragraph?

lesson plan **27** Chaining Information

Objectives

- Students will identify some of the techniques for chaining information.
- Students will recognize such chaining as an important tool in developing ideas and arguments.
- Students will practice applying knowledge of parts of speech.

Procedures

1. You can tell students that they will look at how to manage information in their essays. In particular, they will practice using chaining techniques to link a topic to a previous comment. It might be useful to remind students what topics and comments are.
2. Distribute Handout 27:1.
3. Review the information with students. You could emphasize that the pattern of linking they will be practicing is very important. However, not all sentences should be linked in this way. This is one way to develop parts of an argument. A writer may only link two or three sentences this way in a paragraph. But it is a pattern that is often less intuitive to students. And it is one that should provide a new compositional tool.
4. Distribute Handout 27:2 and review the directions.
5. Have students complete the handout either individually or in small groups.
6. Review their responses.

MATERIALS

Copies of Handout 27:1 and 27:2

ANSWER KEY

Handout 27:2

1. B (nominalization)
2. C (substitution)
3. B (nominalization if focusing on *dark* or *darkness*) or C (substitution)
4. A (repetition)

Handout 27:1 Chaining Information

BACKGROUND FOR STUDENTS

We've looked at three basic topical patterns for organizing information and adhering to the known/new contract: constant, derived, and chained. All three of these patterns are important, and you will certainly use all three in any piece of academic writing.

Of the three patterns, however, the chained pattern is probably the least intuitive. It is also a very important pattern to control. If we introduce a lot of information in our comments but we never take up any of that information in our subsequent topics, we can end up with underdeveloped analysis. Consider this series of sentences from a student's essay.

Hamlet	cannot decide to act.
Known	**New**

↓

He	overthinks everything.
Known	**New**

↓

For example, he	says in his soliloquy, "To be or not to be."
Known	**New**

↓

Hamlet	Is trying tomake up his mind if he wants to live or die.
Known	**New**

By maintaining a constant topic, the ideas of indecision and overthinking are not taken up and developed. A chained topic would be one possible way that the writer might have developed the argument a little more.

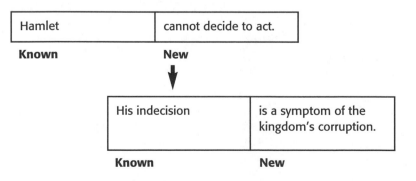

Hamlet	cannot decide to act.
Known	**New**

↓

His indecision	is a symptom of the kingdom's corruption.
Known	**New**

You are now going to be introduced to three strategies for chaining: repetition, nominalization, and summary.

1. Repetition: You've probably been told that repetition is bad. And it's true that you don't want to overdo it. Overrepetition can make a text very monotonous. However, some repetition can be useful in developing ideas. You can take a key word from a comment and repeat it in a following topic.

In *Hamlet,* William Shakespeare	explores many of the **weaknesses** in character that eventually lead to the downfall of an individual.
Known	**New**

↓

All **weaknesses**	are harmful to one's nature, but Hamlet's imperfection is perhaps the most ruinous.
Known	**New**

2. Nominalization: *Nominalization* is a technical term that simply means taking a word that isn't a noun and making it a noun. Often this can be done by adding a suffix like *-ion*, *-ness*, or *-ity*. So a verb like *communicate* can be turned into the noun *communication*. The adjective *polite* can become the noun *politeness*, or the adjective *scarce* can become *scarcity*. Using nominalization, a verb or adjective from a comment can be turned into a noun in the next topic.

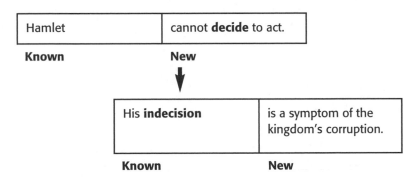

Hamlet	cannot **decide** to act.
Known	**New**

↓

His **indecision**	is a symptom of the kingdom's corruption.
Known	**New**

3. Substitution: To substitute, you can use a synonym for one of the key words in the comment, use a pronoun, or summarize the main idea of the comment. Sometimes writers try to summarize just with the pronoun *this*. Imagine the example reading, "*This* is apparent to even Hamlet. . . ." The reader would be left to figure out what exactly *this* is referring to. When using *this*, it is best, most of the time, to follow it with at least a noun that indicates to the reader what you're discussing.

KEY POINTS

- Academic writing uses all three types of topical patterns: constant, derived, and chained.
- Chaining can be a useful strategy for developing ideas.
- Chaining can be accomplished using repetition, nominalization, or substitution.

IMPORTANT TERMS

nominalization: Converting a word that isn't a noun, like a verb or adjective, into a noun.

Shakespeare	pinpoints **hesitation and over-rationalization** as the source of Hamlet's ultimate ruin.
Known	**New**

↓

Hamlet's **pensiveness**	is a product of the diseased state of the kingdom.
Known	**New**

Handout 27:2 # Chaining Information

Each of the following examples have information connected in a chained pattern. For each one, identify the chaining technique as:

A. Repetition
B. Nominalization
C. Substitution

1. _____

Topic	Comment
Apple	announced Wednesday in its fiscal third-quarter earnings report that it sold 270,000 iPhones in its first two days of release.
The announcement	follows AT&T's report on Tuesday that 146,000 iPhones had been activated in the first 30 hours of sale before the closing of the quarter on June 30. (Pickrell, *Newsday*)

2. _____

Topic	Comment
In a matter of years, Bonds	went from a wiry leadoff hitter with Pittsburgh in 1986 to a bulked-up slugger.
That transformation	is at the heart of his many doubters, who believe Bonds cheated to accomplish his feats and should not be considered the record-holder. (Associated Press, ESPN)

3. _____

Topic	Comment
The appeal of the original *Crow* movie, and the incredible graphic novel upon which it was based,	is the vicious, dark hero who visits his enemies' own brutality back on them without hesitation or remorse.
To cut down on that darkness, even if it's necessary to draw the story out	is to dilute everything that made the film such a cult phenomenon. (DiLeo, IGN)

4. _____

Topic	Comment
Last year, T.I.	was the only rapper to sell more than a million records with his "King" album, an audio tour of life in Atlanta.
That album	debuted at No. 1 on the Billboard 200 charts last spring and sold 522,000 copies in its first week. (Carter, *Detroit Free Press*)

lesson plan 28 Nominalization

MATERIALS

Copies of Handout 28:1

OTHER IDEAS

If you are concerned about students overusing nominalization, have them work with examples that you think are ineffective.

ANSWER KEY

Handout 28:1

1. resentment
2. insignificance
3. consciousness
4. illustration
5. allusion
6. existence
7. induce
8. defy
9. analyze
10. juxtapose

Objectives

- Students will practice nominalization techniques.
- Students will apply their knowledge of parts of speech.
- Students will use vocabulary words relevant to literary analysis.

Procedures

1. You can remind students what *nominalization* means and its role in chaining information. Here they will be doing a quick practice on nominalization before practicing chaining.
2. Distribute Handout 28:1.
3. Review the directions with students. In the directions, I try to highlight the importance of strategic nominalization. Being able to nominalize is an important skill, but it can be overdone. Students need to learn it and experiment with it, but they also need to be aware that it should be done with a purpose, like linking information.
4. Have students complete the handout either individually or in small groups.
5. Review their responses.

Handout 28:1 # Nominalization

Throughout these lessons, I've been trying to emphasize that writing is about making choices—choices in the grammatical system you apply, choices in the words you use, choices in the organization of your sentences.

Nominalization is another one of those choices. I've introduced the technique of nominalization as one way to connect a sentence comment to a subsequent sentence topic. This is an important skill. It helps you organize the flow of information in an essay and allows you to elaborate your ideas.

Many style guides, however, warn against excessive nominalization because some nominalizations can seem too wordy:

> The discussion was about . . .

rather than

> They discussed . . .

In your writing, you need to decide if a nominalization is useful or not. Therefore, you need to be able to both make nouns and unmake them, to both nominalize and unnominalize.

Make the following adjectives and verbs into nouns.
1. resent
2. insignificant
3. conscious
4. illustrate
5. allude
6. exist

Make the following nouns into verbs.
7. inducement
8. defiance
9. analysis
10. juxtaposition

...... **help!** ....

How do I make a nominalization?

Making a noun out of an adjective or verb usually involves the addition of a suffix. Here are some common ones.

For making an adjective a noun:
  -ness
  rude ➤ rudeness
  -ity
  stupid ➤ stupidity
  -ence
  confident ➤ confidence

For making a verb a noun:
  -ion
  act ➤ action
  -ation
  infest ➤ infestation
  -ment
  entertain ➤ entertainment
  -ing
  sing ➤ singing
  -al
  deny ➤ denial
  -ure
  expose ➤ exposure

Instead of adding a suffix, sometimes making a noun requires the dropping of a suffix:

  beautiful ➤ beauty

And sometimes it requires you to do nothing at all:

  change ➤ change

So how do you know if you've ended up with a noun? Remember the form tests? Can it, for example, accept an article (*a/an/the*)? Like *the denial* . . . And remember the function test? Can it be the subject of a verb? Like *the infestation was* . . .

lesson plan 29   Chaining Information, Continued

MATERIALS

Copies of Handout 29:1

OTHER IDEAS

Have students choose paragraphs from their own writing and track the known/new patterns from sentence to sentence. Do they keep to the known/new contract? Do they overrely on the constant pattern? Do they ever chain information?

ANSWER KEY

Handout 29:1

1. His actions . . . (*or* His impulsiveness . . .)
2. His lack of control . . . (*or* recklessness, impetuousness, *and so on*)
3. His audacity . . .
4. His boldness . . . (*or* moment of bravery, daring, *and so on*)
5. These opportunities . . .

Objectives

- Students will practice chaining topics that are linked to a preceding comment.
- Students will apply their knowledge of parts of speech.

Procedures

1. You can tell students that they will complete their work on chaining topics.
2. Distribute Handout 29:1.
3. Review the directions with students. They will compose topics for the missing ones in the second sentence of examples A–C using nominalization, substitution, and repetition.
4. Have students complete the handout either individually or in small groups.
5. Review their responses.

Handout 29:1 # Chaining Information, Continued

Examples A, B, and C are from a student's essay on *Hamlet*. You are going to use chaining techniques (repetition, nominalization, and substitution) to answer the questions that follow.

A.

Topic	Comment
Laertes	acts impulsively.
???	backfire(s), however, leaving him the victim of his own villainy.

B.

Topic	Comment
Hamlet, finding Claudius defenseless and kneeling in prayer,	feels audacious and draws his sword.
???	is cut short, however, by his cowardice and reflection.

C.

Topic	Comment
Time and time again, Hamlet	is presented with opportunities to avenge his father.
???	never reach(es) fruition because Hamlet's rationality outweighs his passion.

1. Use nominalization to compose a chained topic for the second sentence in example A. (Hint: Start with *His* . . .)
2. Use substitution to compose a chained topic for the second sentence in example A.
3. Use nominalization to compose a chained topic for the second sentence in example B. (Hint: Find an adjective to nominalize.)
4. Use substitution to compose a chained topic for the second sentence in example B.
5. Use repetition to compose a chained topic for the second sentence in example C. (Hint: Start with *These* . . .)

Conjunctive Resources and Cohesion

"As relational links, conjunctive resources are incredibly important in both academic writing and testing. Arguments, after all, are developed by demonstrating the relationship of various claims."

Key Points

- Conjunctive resources help texts "hang together" and connect events and propositions.
- Conjunctive resources include coordinating conjunctions, subordinating conjunctions, and conjunctive adverbs.
- The conjunctive resources of speech are different from the conjunctive resources of academic writing.
- Students sometimes use informal spoken resources in their formal writing.
- Students often underuse academic conjunctive resources.

Background for Teachers

In the previous set of lessons, we looked at strategies for organizing information in academic writing. Some of those strategies involved condensing and replicating information through nominalization, substitution, or simple repetition. All of these are important to cohesion—the ways in which a text holds together. Cohesion can be quite various and complex. For example, cohesion is accomplished through the use of thematically related vocabulary as well as though reference, primarily pronouns. Indeed, the complexity of cohesion can sometimes be more interesting to marvel at after a text has been produced (*How do we do that?*) than to think strategically about as we compose. There is, however, one set of cohesive devices that is relatively easy to think about strategically and one that is often underused by students—conjunctive resources.

IMPORTANT TERMS

conjunctive resources: Words or phrases (including coordinating conjunctions, subordinating conjunctions, and conjunctive adverbs) used to logically connect sentences or parts of sentences. Four basic categories of logical relation include addition, comparison, time, and consequence.[9]

Conjunctive resources include coordinating conjunctions, subordinating conjunctions, and conjunctive adverbs (technical terms you may know but that are not crucial for these particular lessons). Conjunctive resources are those words that connect one idea (whether expressed in a sentence or part of a sentence) to another. And, most importantly, they establish the relationship between those ideas. As relational links, conjunctive resources are incredibly important in both academic writing and testing. Arguments, after all, are developed by demonstrating the relationship of various claims.

The conjunctive resources that we all use in speech are very different from those that we need to use in academic writing. For example, two common conjunctions in speech are *and* and *because*. In speech, these conjunctions have many uses. For example, *and* is often used to indicate how two events are related by time, and *because* can be used to link two clauses coordinately, rather than subordinately. (That is, *because* doesn't show a causal link between two propositions, but rather links them more like *and* does.) Sometimes these spoken uses show up in students' writing. Here are two examples from students' essays on *All the Pretty Horses*.

> He ran away with his best friend by the name of Rawlins, **and** they are joined by a younger, more stubborn and sensitive boy named Blevins.

> There were few cattle in that country **because** it was desolate country indeed.

In the first sentence, *and* is used to indicate that the event in the second clause occurs after the event in the first one. To express that relationship using more academic conjunctive resources, the student could have written . . . *and subsequently they are joined*, for example. In the second sentence, the second clause is not necessarily a consequence of the first—desolation doesn't explain the lack of cattle. In this case, the two clauses could be separated into sentences without *because*.

Not only do students use more informal conjunctive resources in their formal academic writing, but they also sometimes do not include logical connections between statements or propositions. Consider, for example, the following paragraph.

> The locusts in *Things Fall Apart* depict the white settlers, who invade and destroy the natural resources of the natives. The locusts eat the crops. They may be viewed as eating their thoughts or beliefs. The white settlers take in their thoughts by converting to them Christianity, which many end up doing. The oracle says, "Other white men were on their way. They were locusts . . . "

Each sentence in this paragraph states a proposition, but none of the propositions are connected explicitly. In the absence of any conjunctive resources, we may very well try to fill in the blanks ourselves as we read: the

ONLINE RESOURCES

Cohesion in Academic Writing
www.services.unimelb.edu.au/llsu/resources/esl/gram003.html

Connective Words
http://unilearning.uow.edu.au/effective/6b.html

second sentence seems to be an example; the third sentence seems to be a symbolic interpretation of the first, and so on.

In these next two lessons, we want to familiarize students with some of the conjunctive resources common in academic writing and give students some practice using those resources.

lesson plan 30 Conjunctive Resources

Objectives

- Students will become familiar with some of the basic properties of conjunctive resources.
- Students will identify words that can express important logical relationships in academic writing.

Procedures

1. Many of the words that we work with in this lesson are often called *transition words* in English classrooms. If you use that terminology, you could begin by asking students for examples of transition words that they use in their academic writing. After the class has generated a short list, you might ask them where they use transition words in their essays. They might say, for example, that they use them in their topic sentences or when introducing a quotation. In fact, these words are important to include at any moment in an essay where you need to indicate to your reader the relationship between things or ideas. They are going to be working with these words so that they can use them effectively in their writing.

2. Distribute Handout 30:1.

3. Review the directions with students. The four categories should be fairly self-explanatory. You might need to emphasize that the category of *comparison* also includes contrast. Also, *consequence* might present a bit of a challenge. In general, *consequence* expresses *how* or *why*. It can show the cause of something, the means by which something happened, the reason something happened, or the condition of something. They can also express a **negative** consequence or **counter** a claim or condition.

4. Have students complete the handout either individually or in small groups.

5. Review students' responses. Students will be able to readily classify most of the words. Some, however, are likely to provoke a variety of responses, in some cases because students may be unfamiliar with the word. In other cases, a word may have multiple uses, or a word may have uses more common to spoken language and uses more preferred in academic writing. For example, most students will probably classify *since* under *time*; however, some students might view it as synonymous with *because* and, therefore, classify under *consequence*. For example:

   Since Sethe denies her past, the past continues to seek Sethe's attention.

   The question, then, would be whether this use of *since* is conventional in the academic register.

MATERIALS

Copies of Handout 30:1

ANSWER KEY

Handout 30:1

T	after
A	again
A	also
CN	although
A	and
T	as soon as
CN	because
CP or CN	but
CN	consequently
CN	despite
T	eventually
T	finally
CP	for example
CP	for instance
A	furthermore
CN	hence
CN or CP	however
A	in addition
CP	in contrast
CP	likewise
A	moreover
CN	nevertheless
A	or
CP	rather than
CP	similarly
T	since
CN	so
T	subsequently
T or CN	then
CN	therefore
CN	thus
A	too
CN	unless
T or CN	when
T or CP	while
CN	yet

Students may have difficulty with words like *although*, words that counter and qualify. They may want to classify such words under *comparison* rather than *consequence*. If students want to argue for a particular classification, that's great. Have the class compose a sample sentence using the word. Ask them to explain the logical link it expresses. Being able to articulate such an explanation is far more important than any particular classification.

Handout 30:1 Conjunctive Resources

Conjunctive resources are simply the words and phrases we use to connect sentences or parts of sentences. Two of the most common conjunctive resources, for example, are *and* and *because*. Conjunctive resources are important in academic writing because they express the relationship between ideas. For example, consider the two sequential statements below from a student's essay on *Beloved*.

> Schoolteacher travels to Ohio to find Sethe twenty-eight days after her escape from slavery.

> Sethe attempts to kill her children instead of returning to Sweet Home.

What is the relationship between them? Are they related by time? If so, you could start the first statement with *when* or the second with *then*. Or are they related by cause and effect? In that case, you could start the first statement with *because* or the second with *so*. The choice here makes a big difference in how the argument is developed.

Just like the known/new contract, the effective use of conjunctive resources is a very important tool in organizing your academic writing.

Conjunctive resources can be put into four categories: **addition**, **comparison**, **time**, and **consequence**. Each of these categories describes a kind of relationship between connected events or ideas. The names of the categories are fairly descriptive. Nonetheless, the table below should help clarify their basic properties.

	Addition	**Comparison**	**Time**	**Consequence**
Logical relationships	adding alternating	comparing contrasting	ordering sequencing	explaining concluding countering
Example	and	similarly	then	because

For each of the conjunctions below, identify it as belonging either to (A) addition, (CP) comparison, (T) time, or (CN) consequence.

_____	after	_____	for example	_____	similarly
_____	again	_____	for instance	_____	since
_____	also	_____	furthermore	_____	so
_____	although	_____	hence	_____	subsequently
_____	and	_____	however	_____	then
_____	as soon as	_____	in addition	_____	therefore
_____	because	_____	in contrast	_____	thus
_____	but	_____	likewise	_____	too
_____	consequently	_____	moreover	_____	unless
_____	despite	_____	nevertheless	_____	when
_____	eventually	_____	or	_____	while
_____	finally	_____	rather than	_____	yet

lesson plan **31** Conjunctive Resources, Continued

MATERIALS

Copies of Handout 31:1

ANSWER KEY

Handout 31:1

Students answers will vary, but here are some possibilities:

1. *Consequently* (or *Yet*)
2. *despite*
3. *because*
4. *When*
5. *But* (or *However*)
6. *For example*
7. *therefore* (or a resource of time like *eventually* or *finally*)
8. *Subsequently*
9. *eventually*

Students might notice that various temporal resources can be interchanged like *subsequently*, *eventually*, and sometimes *finally*.

Objectives

• Students will practice the effective use of conjunctive resources.

• Students will expand their repertoires of conjunctive resources.

Procedures

1. You can begin by telling students that they will finish their work with conjunctive resources (or transition words).

2. Distribute copies of Handout 31:1, and review the directions with students. If there are other conjunctive resources or transition words that you would like students to practice, add them to the list.

3. Have students complete the handout individually.

4. Review their responses. Students will have a variety of answers. You can have students compare their answers to others' and make arguments for why they selected particular words. For example, some students may have a conjunction of *time* rather than *consequence* for the first blank. How does this change the relationship of those sentences? How does it change the argument? A variety of responses will work for most of the blanks. Students' rationale for choosing a word or a word from a particular classification is the most important part of the exercise.

Handout 31:1 # Conjunctive Resources, Continued

Below is the list of conjunctive resources that you worked with in the previous exercise. Use any of these words (or any other transition word you think is appropriate) to fill in the blanks in the following paragraph from a student's essay. Pay close attention to what the missing words are linking. Figuring out their logical relationship will help you choose the most effective word.

Addition (adding, alternating)	Comparison (comparing, contrasting)	Time (ordering, sequencing)	Consequence (explaining, concluding, countering)
again, also, and, furthermore, in addition, moreover, or	for example, for instance, in contrast, likewise, rather than, similarly	after, as soon as, eventually, finally, since, subsequently, then, when, while	although, because, but, consequently, despite, hence, however, nevertheless, so, therefore, thus, unless, yet

To protect her children, Sethe becomes the judge between two evils and finds that security in death is better than slavery. (1) _____ twenty years after the incident, Sethe's home is still haunted by the presence of the "crawling-already?" baby. The spirit is melancholy, vengeful, and prone to fits of rage when craving attention from the inhabitants of 124. Sethe and Denver both welcome this haunting presence, (2) _____ the havoc it raises, (3) _____ both are convinced of its right to be in their home with them. (4) _____ Beloved—Sethe's symbolic past—enters 124 in human form, she is immediately drawn in and protected by Sethe. (5) _____ as their relationship deepens, Beloved quickly makes it apparent that she is in command. (6) _____ she only needed to say, "'Do it,' and Sethe complied." Her presence, (7) _____, transforms Sethe from a proud, confident woman into an apologetic, cowering skeleton of her former self. (8) _____ Sethe becomes so "loaded with the past and hungry for more," she is "not interested in the future." Her sole desire becomes so bent upon pleasing Beloved that she crowds out Denver's needs, and (9) _____, her own as well.

Verb Processes

Key Points

- Verb processes can be divided into four basic groups: (1) doing, (2) sensing and thinking, (3) saying, and (4) being.

- Academic writing makes use of all four types of processes; however, academic subjects use these processes in different ways and in different proportions.

- In academic writing, processes are sometimes used metaphorically with concepts, abstractions, or figurative actors as participants.

Background for Teachers

We have looked at the basic structure of sentences and clauses, and we have looked at strategies for connecting and organizing sentences and clauses. Now, we want to look at the processes of sentences and clauses—the verbs that are their engines.

In the previous lessons, we were able to divide conjunctive resources into categories based on their functions. And we can do the same thing with verbs. Verbs can be categorized according to the type of process that they enact: (1) doing, (2) sensing and thinking, (3) saying, and (4) being.[10]

Verbs of doing enact material and physical process: *chemicals **react**, mountains **form**,* and so on. Here is an example from a student's paper on *Pride and Prejudice*.

> When Bingley **leaves** for London and **does not return**, Jane **follows** him in hopes of an explanation.

Verbs of sensing and thinking enact mental processes: *she **wonders**, he **saw**,* and so on. Here is an example from that same paper.

> Although Jane logically **knows** that marriage to a class higher than her own is unlikely, she **cannot pretend** that she has no interest in Bingley.

Verbs of saying enact communicative process: *the author **argues**, scholars **claim**,* and so on. These verbs frequently, though not necessarily, come before quotations.

> "In the previous lessons, we were able to divide conjunctive resources into categories based on their functions. And we can do the same thing with verbs. Verbs can be categorized according to the type of process that they enact."

Elizabeth **states** that the "greatest misfortune of all" would be to "find a man agreeable whom one is determined to hate."

Finally, verbs of being enact relational or existential processes: *the solution is*, *the character seems*, and so on. They can identify or characterize the subject.

When Bingley throws his first ball at Netherfield, he **appears** quite enamored with Jane.

Academic writing, of course, makes use of all four types of processes. However, academic subjects use these processes in different ways and in different proportions. Writing in history, for example, relies a great deal on doing verbs to recount events and on some being verbs to set out the conditions surrounding those events. Writing in science also uses doing verbs to narrate procedures or processes, but leans heavily on being verbs for definitions and conclusions.

In the English classroom, writing about literature makes extensive use of doing verbs in the recounting of plot as well as sensing and thinking verbs in the description of characters' psychological states. Writing about literature, however, also relies on saying verbs for quotation and attribution and, importantly, being verbs for definition, analysis, and conclusion.

In addition, as student writers advance, they may begin to use doing and sensing and thinking verbs metaphorically. Verbs that we may generically think of as having human or tangible participants instead have concepts, abstractions, or figurative actors as participants.

Eliot's poem **considers** the spiritual death of human beings as all too common.

We touched on the importance of abstraction in our examination of topics and comments. Here, I want to directly address the use of abstracted participants because it is a crucial skill for composing analysis.

In general, I want students to develop greater awareness of the verbs that they choose and the work that those verbs can do in their essays.

lesson plan 32 Types of Verb Processes

MATERIALS

Copies of Handout 32:1

ANSWER KEY

Handout 32:1

S	agree
ST	analyze
B	appear
D	approach
S	argue
B	be
D	coerce
D (or S)	demonstrate
S	discuss
D (or S)	encourage
D (or S)	establish
S	exaggerate
ST	examine
D	expand
S	explain
ST	fascinate
D (or S)	illustrate
ST	imagine
ST	observe
D	possess
D	produce
S (or D)	respond
D (or S)	reveal
B	seem
S	state
S	suggest
D	undermine
D	use

Objectives

- Students will become familiar with some of the basic verb processes.
- Students will identify verbs that can express important processes in academic writing.

Procedures

1. You can begin by telling students that they will work with verbs similar to the way they just worked with conjunctive resources. If necessary, remind students what a verb is.
2. Distribute copies of Handout 32:1, and review the directions with students. If there are other verbs that you would like students to practice, add them to the list.
3. Have students complete the handout individually or in small groups.
4. Review their responses. There may be some variation in students' answers. You can have students compare their answers to others' and make arguments for why they selected particular categories. For example, some students may have *encourage* as a saying rather than a doing verb. Why did they choose that particular category? Can they come up with a sample sentence that justifies a particular categorization? Because most of these verbs have several definitions, a variety of responses could be argued for many of them. Students' rationales for choosing a particular classification are the most important part of the exercise.

Some of these verbs have multiple definitions. For such verbs, students could argue for different categories. Also, verbs are often used metaphorically (for example, *she established her argument . . .*); thus, verbs of doing frequently stand in for mental or communicative processes. The metaphorical use of some verbs may complicate students' categorization and is a point we will turn to in the next lesson. As with the conjunctive resources, the emphasis here is on students' reasoning rather than a particular answer.

Handout 32:1 **Types of Verb Processes**

In looking at conjunctive resources, we were able to categorize them according to the logical relationship they express (addition, comparison, time, or consequence). We can categorize verbs in a similar way. Verbs are the engines of sentences and clauses, and they enact various kinds of processes.

These processes can be divided into four basic categories: (1) doing, (2) sensing and thinking, (3) saying, and (4) being. Verbs of doing are associated with physical (though not necessarily human) action, sensing and thinking verbs with mental activity, saying verbs with communication, and being verbs with existence. Below is a table to help you understand the basic properties of the different categories.

	Doing	**Sensing and Thinking**	**Saying**	**Being**
Description	Verbs of material and physical action.	Verbs associated with the senses or with mental activity.	Verbs of communication. Often these verbs come before quotations.	Verbs of identification, characterization, or comparison.
Examples (verbs in bold)	Like a lot of big-ticket productions "Rush Hour 3" **will flood** into theaters this weekend . . . (*New York Times*) Barry Bonds **swung**, **took** a half-dozen steps and **clapped** his hands. (CNN)	Fifth-season finalist Kellie Pickler **understands** the fleeting nature of pop culture. (*Seattle Times*) But I clearly **remember** that moment and **wondering** about his daughter, Lisa Marie, whom I **must have seen** on TV once or twice. (*Chicago Sun-Times*)	"Nobody **can explain** this song, not even me," he **told** the crowd. (*Rolling Stone*) Beckham **announced** that he would not play in the team's match against Toronto FC on Sunday, Aug. 5. (*San Jose Mercury News*)	USC **is** the preseason team to beat. (ESPN) Woods **became** the first major champion in seven tries to make a par on the 72nd hole at Southern Hills. (*Globe and Mail*)

The following list of verbs has been compiled from students' essays. For each of the verbs, identify it as belonging either to (D) doing, (ST) sensing and thinking, (S) saying, or (B) being.

_____ to agree   _____ to explain

_____ to analyze   _____ to fascinate

_____ to appear   _____ to illustrate

_____ to approach   _____ to imagine

_____ to argue   _____ to observe

_____ to be   _____ to possess

_____ to coerce   _____ to produce

_____ to demonstrate   _____ to respond

_____ to discuss   _____ to reveal

_____ to encourage   _____ to seem

_____ to establish   _____ to state

_____ to exaggerate   _____ to suggest

_____ to examine   _____ to undermine

_____ to expand   _____ to use

lesson plan **33** Abstract Participants of Verbs

Objectives

- Students will recognize the difference between abstract and physical participants in verb processes.
- Students will work with verbs—other than verbs of being—that can work, metaphorically or otherwise, with abstract participants.

Procedures

1. You might start by telling students that they will expand their study of verbs to include not just the verb itself, but also participants in the process that a verb enacts.

2. Distribute copies of Handout 33:1 and review the directions with students. There is a mention of nominalization in the directions. You might remind students what that is. Also, in the help! column, there is a brief summary of subjects and objects. If students are confused about identifying participants, you can go over those concepts.

3. Have students complete the handout individually or in small groups.

4. Review their responses. After the review, you could ask students when, in their essays, they might be expected to use more abstract participants. Abstractions will tend to show up most frequently in their analysis, as well as at the beginning and end of paragraphs and in introductions and conclusions. You also might note that none of these examples contains verbs of being. Being verbs are very useful, but they are often the default verb when writing about abstractions. There is nothing wrong with using being verbs, but they can be overused, and there are other options. This is a topic we will tackle in the next lesson.

MATERIALS

Copies of Handout 33:1

ANSWER KEY

Handout 33:1

1. A
   verb: *emphasize* (saying)
   participants: *the allusions to the novella*; *human suffering and emptiness*
2. A
   verb: *create* (doing)
   participants: *both the physical and spiritual suffering of the characters in Conrad and Eliot's works*; *"hollow men"*
3. P
   verb: *form* (doing)
   participants: *the men*; *prayers to broken stone*
4. A
   verb: *uncovers* (doing)
   participants: *Marlowe's fascination*; *his true nature*
5. P
   verb: *ventures* (doing)
   participants: *Kurtz*
   Note that students may want to include *into the jungle* as a participant. The jungle is the location of the venturing but not a participant. This is a prepositional phrase rather than a verb object.
6. A or P
   verb: *considers* (sensing and thinking)
   participants: *Eliot's poem*; *the spiritual death of human beings*
   This is a borderline case. Certainly, a student could make the case that *the poem* is a physical thing. Conversely, a student could argue that *spiritual death* is abstract. In addition, *considering* is being used metaphorically, as this is a cognitive faculty that poems don't possess. Thus, *the poem* takes on an abstract quality.

Handout 33:1 # Abstract Participants of Verbs

It is important to recognize not only the roles various verbs can play in our writing but also the participants in those verb processes (the subjects and objects of verbs). Many times, the participants are predictable. In writing about literature, for example, there will certainly be instances in which characters are the participants.

Sometimes, however, the participants may not be quite so obvious. In academic writing, is not uncommon for participants to be more abstract, particularly when the writer is composing analysis. Participants can be ideas or attributes of people or things. And the processes they participate in can be ones that we may generically think of as having human or tangible participants.

For example, *to damage* is a verb of doing.

> A line of heavy thunderstorms **damaged** buildings, tore the roof off of a high school and downed trees in other parts of the state. (Associated Press, *USA Today*)

However, abstractions, ideas, or characteristics can be participants of *to damage* as well.

> His poor judgment **has** already **damaged** his credibility. (Levy, *The Wall Street Journal*)

In the first example, there are physical participants (*A line of heavy thunderstorms* and *buildings*). In the second, there are abstract participants (*His poor judgment* and *credibility*) Note that these are both nominalizations (of *to judge* and *credible*). Often these types of participants are nominalizations, but they don't have to be.

Each of the six following quotations have been taken from a student's paper comparing *Heart of Darkness* and "The Hollow Men." For each sentence, do the following:

- Circle the verb and identify it as doing, sensing and thinking, saying, or being.
- Underline the participant(s) in the verb process.
- Identify the participant(s) as physical (P) or abstract (A).

1. ____ The allusions to the novella emphasize human suffering and emptiness.

2. ____ Both the physical and spiritual suffering of the characters in Conrad and Eliot's works

   create "hollow men."

3. ____ The men, instead, "form prayers to broken stone."

4. ____ Marlowe's fascination uncovers his true nature.

5. ____ Kurtz ventures into the jungle.

6. ____ Eliot's poem considers the spiritual death of human beings as all too common.

help!

How do I recognize the subject or object of a verb?

The **subject** is the actor of a verb. It is a noun, pronoun, or noun phrase and is the verb's doer. In declarative sentences (as opposed to questions) the subject comes before the verb.

The **object** (or objects) is the noun, pronoun, or noun phrase that the verb acts upon. It is the receiver and in declarative sentences comes after the verb.

Some verbs take objects (**transitive** verbs) and some don't (**intransitive** verbs). *Run*, for example, is normally intransitive: *She ran. She* is the subject, but there is no object. However, *run* can be transitive: *She ran the office. The office* is the object.

The ability of verbs to be both transitive and intransitive is not uncommon.

lesson plan 34 Verbs of Being

Objectives

- Students will work with alternatives to the verb *to be*.
- Students will practice editing strategies.

Procedures

1. You can tell students that they will turn their attention to the verb *to be*, specifically, and its use and overuse in academic writing.

2. Distribute copies of Handout 34:1.

3. Review the directions with students. It might be worth emphasizing that *to be* doesn't need to be avoided. It is necessary in academic writing. However, students need to pay attention to the potential for overusing it.

4. Have students complete the handout individually or in small groups. If students have difficulty, you might do the first one together as a class.

5. Review their responses. Students may end up changing the verbs with no discernable pattern. However, if a large number of students change particular verbs or leave particular verbs alone, it would be interesting to discuss what in those grammatical environments invited either change or preservation.

MATERIALS

Copies of Handout 34:1

OTHER IDEAS

The passive voice can be an interesting topic. Generally, we are taught to avoid it, but it isn't always bad. When might we use it? How might it serve the known/new contract or information structure?

ANSWER KEY

Handout 34:1

Answers will vary, but here are some possibilities:

1. . . . three children torment her despite . . .
2. . . . Sethe becomes the judge . . .
   or
   . . . Sethe chooses between two evils . . .
3. . . . death prevails over slavery . . .
4. . . . "crawling already?" baby haunts Sethe's . . .
5. The spirit appears melancholy . . .
6. . . . Sethe and Denver accept this haunting . . .
7. . . . both Sethe and Denver recognize its right . . .
8. . . . to live in their home . . .
   or
   . . . to inhabit their home . . .

The verbs students change and those that they leave should make for an interesting discussion. #1 seems like a good candidate for change as does #6, and #3 seems like one that could be left alone.

Handout 34:1 # Verbs of Being

Verbs of being are very important in academic writing. We can use them to create definitions, and to identify things, people, and ideas, and we can use them to assign characteristics. They allow us to say what something *is, seems,* or *becomes.* Verbs of being, then, are an indispensable resource for expository or analytical writing.

However, it is common to rely too much on one particular verb: *to be.* It's not that we shouldn't use *to be.* We have to. But we should be judicious in how and when we use it. In writing, we are always making choices.

Below is an excerpt from a student's paper on *Beloved.* In this excerpt, the writer excessively leans on the verb *to be,* using it eight times in five sentences.

Choose four of the eight instances of *to be* and rewrite them using different verbs. In some cases, you may be able to substitute a different verb of being, in others you may have to rework the sentence and use another type of verb—one of doing, saying, or sensing and thinking.

Be prepared to defend your choices.

> Sethe's memory of murdering one daughter and almost killing her other three children is[1] a torment despite her belief that she acts out of love because she "couldn't let . . . any of em live under schoolteacher." To protect her children, Sethe is[2] the judge between two evils and finds that security in death is[3] better than slavery. Now, twenty years after the incident, Sethe's home is[4] still haunted by the presence of the "crawling-already?" baby. The spirit is[5] melancholy, vengeful, and prone to fits of rage when craving attention from the inhabitants of 124. Despite the havoc it raises, this haunting presence is[6] accepted because both Sethe and Denver are[7] convinced of its right to be[8] in their home with them.

Academic Language Review

Background for Teachers

In our examination of academic language we have looked at the following.

- topic/comment structure
- the known/new contract
- conjunctive resources and cohesion
- verb processes

Through our study, observations that we have made about writing in the English classroom include:

- There needs to be a balance between complex and simple topics.
- In analytical writing, it is sometimes important for ideas, concepts, abstractions, and nominalizations to appear in topics or to be participants in verb processes.
- Most of the time, known information should precede new information.
- The organization of information can follow a number of different patterns, but any pattern should match the purpose of the writing.
- Chaining is an important strategy in analytical writing.
- Doing, sensing and thinking, saying, and being verbs are all used in academic writing, though academic subjects use these processes in different ways and in different proportions.
- Being verbs are crucial to definition, analysis, and conclusion, but novice writers can sometimes overrely on the verb *to be*.

Although what we have covered is not exhaustive (and serves only as a complement to, not a replacement for, students' ideas and creativity), it can help students think strategically about the language that they use in their essays. It can also help students and teachers troubleshoot some common issues. What does it mean that an essay needs development? (New information is introduced that is never taken up in a subsequent topic.) Or doesn't flow? (The information structure isn't working, or conjunctive resources are underutilized.) Or lacks

"Although what we have covered is not exhaustive, it can help students think strategically about the language that they use in their essays. It can also help students and teachers troubleshoot some common issues."

ONLINE RESOURCES

Features of Academic Writing

www.uefap.com/writing/writfram.htm

Effective Writing

http://unilearning.uow.edu.au/main.html

focus? (The topics are unconnected either by information or conjunctive resources.)

In the final lesson, we will examine some of these very issues. Students will analyze part of a student's essay that isn't particularly successful. Using some of the tools they have learned, they will try to deduce why, exactly, this particular piece of writing doesn't work.

OTHER IDEAS

If you have students analyze topic/comment and known/new structure in their own essays, you can add detail to their analysis by having them perform the same processes with each clause rather than each sentence.

Thus, sentences that have subordinate or coordinate clauses would be broken up.

When Bingley	leaves for London and does not return,	Jane	follows him in hopes of an explanation.

Although this is an advanced task, it will more accurately represent the flow and development of information in students' writing. In addition, it will help students recognize the subordination, coordination, and embedding of clauses, which are important structures in academic writing.

lesson plan 35 Academic Language Review

Objectives

- Students will review their knowledge of academic language.

Procedures

1. You may start by telling students that they will review their work with academic language. You may need to quickly go over topic/comment and known/new.
2. Distribute copies of Handout 35:1, and review the directions with students.
3. The goal is to have students try to reconstruct the disassembled paragraph. Have them complete the activity either individually or in small groups. This is not a particularly successful paragraph, which may make some of the ordering difficult.
4. When they are done, as a class, make a tally on the board of what sentences they thought went first, second, and so on and how many students chose each sentence? In this way, you should be able to determine where students agreed and where they disagreed, what sentences were easy to place and what sentences were difficult.
5. Discuss with students whether they found ordering the paragraph easy or difficult and why. Were there particular sentences they found more challenging to place than others? What made them easy or difficult to place? How did the known/new structure help or hinder this task? What about the use of conjunctive resources?
6. Finally, check their identification of topics and discuss them. Are topics mostly simple or complex? Abstract or physical? Is there enough balance between simple and complex topics? Where does the writer's choice of topics make this paragraph easier or more difficult to put in order, more or less effective? Because the topics are fairly unchanging and are mostly about things rather than concepts, some of these sentences can feel a little interchangeable? Also, there are two topics that seem out of place: *You* and *Conrad*.

OTHER IDEAS

This activity can be easier if the students actually cut the sentences into strips and physically try to reorder them.

MATERIALS

Copies of Handout 35:1

ANSWER KEY

Handout 35:1

The topics are as follows:
A. The flow of the river
B. You
C. Fog
D. Conrad
E. The symbol of fog
F. As much of an access route the river may be, it
G. The river itself, where much of the novel takes place
H. Being caught in the fog
I. It
J. The river
K. It

The actual order of the paragraph is:

1.	E	7.	F
2.	C	8.	A
3.	H	9.	K
4.	B	10.	J
5.	G	11.	D
6.	I		

Because this paragraph is not entirely successful, answers will be quite varied.

In part, the paragraph suffers because themes are largely divided into two groups: those about the fog and those about the river. There is, however, no obvious link between the two.

Also, the first sentence (E) introduces *the darkness theme* as new information in the comment, but that comment is never taken up elsewhere in the paragraph. Much of what follows is about movement and access, which is not explicitly connected to the theme of *darkness*.

Finally, there is almost no use of conjunctive resources.

Handout 35:1 # Academic Language Review

The following a paragraph is from a student's essay on *Heart of Darkness*. It has been broken up into individual sentences that have been put out of order.

First, circle all of the topics for sentences A–K.

Then, using what you've learned about academic language including topic/comment and known/new structure, try to put the sentences back in order by putting the letter of the sentence you think goes first next to #1, second next to #2, and so on. Note those places where you have difficulty rearranging the paragraph. What is the problem? What would make this paragraph work better?

A. The flow of the river seems to handicap the colonists as they enter and help them as they try to leave.

B. You do not know where you are, and you do not know where you are going.

C. Fog obscures and distorts a person's ability to see and make decisions.

D. Conrad states, "Going up the river was like traveling back to the earliest beginnings of the world."

E. The symbol of fog enhances the darkness theme given by Conrad.

F. As much of an access route the river may be, it may also be viewed as a barrier, trying to keep the Europeans out of Africa.

G. The river itself, where much of the novel takes place, is a symbol that is key to the setting in *The Heart of Darkness.*

H. Being caught in the fog gives you no sense of direction.

I. It is the main access route for the Europeans to Africa.

J. The river keeps them physically off of their land, where they are not wanted.

K. It signifies the natives not wanting the colonists in their world.

1. _____
2. _____
3. _____
4. _____
5. _____
6. _____
7. _____
8. _____
9. _____
10. _____
11. _____

Making the Lessons Your Own

INTRODUCTION

In Other Words lays out some fundamental principles of language study. It provides students with examples of linguistic features such as *like* and *ain't*, then asks students to find patterns in the use of those features—to induce grammatical rules. One primary purpose of these activities is to help students better understand how English works and to apply that new awareness to their academic writing. The latter half of the book guides students in such applications.

In designing the lessons, I have tried to keep them short in an effort to ease the time demands on teachers and make their implementation less taxing. Of course, there are trade-offs in opting for more streamlined lessons. Language can be an enormously engaging subject of study (Lynne Truss, after all, made *Eats, Shoots and Leaves* a best seller) and a complex one. The lessons offer an introduction and an approach to this complexity, but they are a beginning.

For teachers interested in including more language and grammar study in their classrooms, I hope that the book serves as a springboard and a framework for creating their own lessons. In the book, the text boxes labeled "Other Ideas" offer suggestions for extending students' learning through additional lessons. In this chapter, I would like to address in more detail three areas of possible extension or application that, I think, can be particularly challenging: discussing the politics of English variation, integrating academic language awareness into the writing process and, finally, authoring assessments.

DISCUSSING THE POLITICS OF ENGLISH VARIATION

In *English with an Accent*, Rosina Lippi-Green observes that our manner and style of speaking is one of the most powerful ways we advertise who we are. Like the clothes people wear, we interpret speech as a form of self-presentation and

CONTENTS

use it to judge people's education and character. Often, these judgments happen without our really being conscious of them.

This connection between language and identity has a very long history in the English-speaking world, as I note in the book's Introduction. In 1752, Samuel Johnson railed against "colloquial barbarisms" and "licentious idioms" as a source of linguistic and, therefore, moral corruption. In *Pygmalion*, Henry Higgins declares that Eliza's cockney English is "depressing and disgusting," a debasement that makes her nothing more that a "bilious pigeon." A 1947 guide for teaching actors to speak various American regional dialects suggests that "Southerners are, at once, emotionally violent yet physically indolent, provincial yet worldly wise, educated yet illogical, genteel yet barbarous," that poor Southerners are "slow to thought and slow to speech but quick to violence" and that New Yorkers are "hurried and unfriendly," "frequently opinionated," and "sentimental"—and the guide suggests that all of these characteristics are transmitted through people's patterns of speech (Herman and Herman 1947). We might look on such generalizations now as offensive and dated. Yet, it is still not uncommon to hear speakers of Southern American English describe Northern speech as nasally, harsh, or grating or, conversely, to hear speakers of Northern varieties describe Southern speech as sweet-sounding or languid, and for such opinions to stand in for assessments of Northerners' brusqueness and Southerners' unhurried charm.

When we talk about language, then, sometimes we are using language as a proxy to talk about other things, and, again, our judgments often operate below the level of consciousness. Discussing the social judgments that are made based on speakers' language use can be complicated and emotional. This is particularly true when race and class are implicated in the relationship between language and identity, as they can be in evaluations of features like habitual *be* or *ain't*. People, for example, can be upset simply by the name that most linguists use for the dialect of which habitual *be* is a feature—African American English (a variety popularly referred to as *Ebonics*, which is a termed coined in social psychology not linguistics). Those linguists who use the term use it because that variety evolved in African American communities. However, I have heard students and teachers object to the term because they feel that it implies all African Americans speak the variety (which, of course, is not true) or that only African Americans speak the variety (which is not true either). That just the act of naming can evoke such discomfort illustrates how fraught social and political discussions of language can be.

For teachers using *In Other Words*, the social and political power of language raises some important questions: Should I have discussions with my students about the social implications of language variety? And how can I conduct such discussions most effectively? My answer to the first question would be "no," a teacher does not have to have such a discussion to effectively implement the lessons. First, I think engaging in these kinds of discussions is dependent on the interests of a teacher. If a teacher is inclined to pursue these topics, then I think that they can be wonderfully productive and exciting. If a teacher is not so inclined or is apprehensive, then wading into these issues is not likely to have a constructive outcome. Second, I do not think that such discussions are required because students are not equally ready to examine the social valuations related to language. As I have said already, these examinations can be complex and emotional. Students differ in their ability and willingness to engage these topics. Determining how a particular class might respond is a decision best left to individual teachers.

If teachers are not inclined to pursue social issues related to language variation, they can follow some fairly straightforward guidelines to direct classroom work during the lessons. Though the lessons in the book touch on social issues at times (during the dictionary lessons, for example), they are principally focused on developing students' grammatical knowledge and awareness. During the lessons, however, a student might say something like "*Ain't* isn't even a real word. It just means you don't have an education," or "People who use habitual *be* should speak properly."

If comments of this kind arise, and you don't want to explore some of assumptions that underlie them, you can acknowledge the link between language and social judgments while refocusing students on the primary work at hand:

> It is certainly true that people judge other people based on the way that they speak. Right now, though, we're working on figuring out how these things work. Whether or not we use a particular feature, whether or not we like it, these features are governed by grammatical rules, which allow people to communicate with each other. Figuring out these rules helps us better understand how the English language works. If we can do that, we can be more deliberate about some of the choices that we make in our academic writing.

Something like that anyway. The general idea is that the book is designed to provide teachers and students with information about the grammatical workings of English and to let users of the book make conscious social choices for themselves.

What, however, if a teacher *is* interested in the relationship between language and identity and the social valuations attributed to linguistic features and language variety? Questions such as:

- Why is *ain't* often considered uneducated?
- Why don't people who use the same language speak the same way?

- Is it fair to ask speakers of Vernacular varieties to code-switch into Standard English?
- Does code-switching alter speakers' perceptions of themselves?

Such questions may arise in the routine course of implementing the lessons. Teachers may wish to pursue these topics organically as they crop up, if they have the time and inclination to do so. In that case, I would suggest that teachers can moderate these discussions as they would with a potentially charged book like *Beloved, Night,* or *The Adventures of Huckleberry Finn*: Make sure students are respectful of each other and don't let the conversation stray too far afield—commonsense principles. Also, similar to literary analysis, these questions do not have simple, pithy answers. Students may respond in ways that are more or less thoughtful, that are more or less insightful, but not in ways that are obviously correct or incorrect.

Using Articles and Quotations

If teachers have an interest in designing their own lessons for exploring language and identity, I would first suggest that teachers structure their lessons around specific artifacts. In most instances, it is likely to be more productive to have students respond to a concrete text like a quotation or an article from a newspaper that link language and identity (Brent Staples' "Last Train from Oakland," for example[11]) than to pose abstract questions to students. Activities like these can be organized as informal, individual writing assignments or as more ordered group activities. So, a teacher might have students compose reader-response journal entries to Staples, for example, or have small groups of students carefully analyze the structure of his argument.

How, then, does one find good texts or artifacts with which to work? Finding interesting texts that deal with language and identity is surprisingly easy. People use language to make judgments about other people all the time—and they write about their judgments in editorials, on blogs, on message boards, in wikis. To give you an idea as to how ubiquitous such judgments are, let me relay a quick anecdote. I like college football and spend probably more time than I should following my favorite team on several blogs and message boards. At one point, the team was trying to recruit a future quarterback and two players were expressing interest—one a high school senior and the other a junior. Both players were top-rated, and fans spent a lot of energy fretting over the possibility of their coming to the university. In an online debate about the relative merits of the two players, one message board commentator suggested that, after hearing interviews with the players, he thought that the younger player, the high school junior, would be a better fit for the university and a better quarterback. His assessment was not based on what the players said in their interviews but how they talked. Underlying this assessment was a belief that speaking a more standard variety was indicative not just of the prospective students' education but also their ability to fit into a college campus and, even more remarkably, their skill at playing quarterback.

If you're not in a hurry, one way to find these kinds of artifacts is to keep your eyes open as you read the paper or read online. If you want to create assignments more quickly, you can find references to articles in the "Online Resources" sidebars in the book. You might also Google key terms like *Ebonics*, *slang*, or *teenage slang*—and, if you are looking for more formal texts, you can use Google's "Search News" feature to restrict the results to news-related sites. Other resources for readings are *Language Awareness* by Paul Eschholz, Alfred Rosa, and Virginia Clark, William Safire's "On Language" column in the *New York Times*, and Barbara Wallraff's "Word Court" column in the *Atlantic Monthly*. Finally, you might have students find their own examples of texts in which writers make judgments of people based on their language use.

Using Word Histories

Word histories can also be designed as an activity that connects language study with academic writing practice. A word history generally combines information about the origins of a word with analysis (supported by quotations illustrating actual use) of how a word's meaning and use have evolved. Word history papers can be short (for example, a page) or longer (three pages). Longer assignments may require students to do more research, even conduct interviews with people on their reactions to the words about which the students are writing. These assignments tend to work best when students either choose or are given different words to research. An example of an assignment prompt would be as follows:[12]

> At the beginning of the semester, you "adopted" two words. Now, you will choose one of your adopted words and write a short paper about that word. If your word can be used as multiple parts of speech, you are responsible only for the one use that you have adopted. Your paper should be about five hundred words long and will include each of the following parts:
> I.   First, you will look up the history of your word in the *Oxford English Dictionary* (*OED*)and you will summarize (not copy!) the origins of your word. When did the word originate? In what language? Describe any changes to word's meaning over time (for example, *girl* used to refer to a child of either gender). Be sure to update any new meanings your word has developed that may not be in the *OED*. (Is the current meaning of *swag* as free stuff, for example, in there?)

II. Second, you will write about what your word means. What are its different denotations and connotations? In order to do this, you must look up your word in two different dictionaries (neither of which can be the *OED*). Compare and contrast their entries. Next, interview three people and ask them for their definitions of the word. Are they the same? Different? How do they compare to the dictionary definitions? Finally, find three quotations that illustrate the meaning(s) of the word that you are claiming.

III. Third, you will describe some of the grammatical properties of your word. What part of speech is it? If it is a noun, can it be counted or not? Can it be singular and plural? Is the plural form regular? If it is a verb, does it take the regular past tense ending? If it is an adjective, does it have comparative and superlative forms? Does it usually appear in attributive position, predicative position, or both?

One way to combine language and identity examination with a word history assignment would be to brainstorm words that are shibboleths—words that hearers strongly associate with particular social characteristics or groups. *Ain't*, for example, can be a shibboleth associated with education or intelligence. Similarly, *y'all* (or *ya'll*) can be a shibboleth of Southern American speech. After the class generates a list of shibboleths, students can divvy up the words and compose their histories.

In order to carry out a word history assignment successfully, as the preceding assignment prompt suggests, access to the *OED* is an extremely valuable resource. Unfortunately, not many schools have access to the *OED*. Check the local library and if they don't have access, find out what etymology resources they do have. For an example of a word history, you might look at "Hoosiers" by Geoffrey Nunberg,[13] which appears in his collection *The Way We Talk Now* and which he posted on LinguistList.org. You can also check Merriam-Webster's Word.Com, which has some shorter ones.

Integrating Academic Language Awareness into the Writing Process

Without question, improving students' academic writing is difficult. It is probably one of the most complex challenges that educators are asked to tackle. Though the techniques that I present in the latter sections of *In Other Words* (topic/comment, the known/new contract, verb processes, and conjunctive resources) are not how most English teachers in the United States are accustomed to approaching grammar and composition, they have proven to be effective at improving students' academic writing in places like Australia. In order for these techniques to have a positive impact on students' writing, however, they cannot be restricted to lessons in the book but must be integrated into classroom writing processes. A teacher, for example, could not simply teach the lessons, tell students to hang on to the handouts and, then, reasonably expect any change in students' subsequent work.

Improvement takes time and effort, and there is no magic bullet, no miracle shortcut, for getting students to write well. If teachers are interested in and committed to the approaches to academic writing presented in the book, however, these approaches can be an important and productive component in a writing program.

In order for students to grasp how something like the known/new contract can improve their writing, they need many opportunities to practice applying the concept. One way to provide such opportunities would be to integrate the concepts presented in the book into the writing process. The writing process is generally presented as comprising five steps.

1. Prewriting/invention
2. Writing/drafting
3. Revising
4. Editing/proofing
5. Publishing

Analyzing Topics and Comments

The kinds of activities that are introduced in the book can comfortably be made a part of the revising stage. After composing a draft of a paper, for example, students could circle all of the sentence topics in their first body paragraph. (With all of these activities, I would recommend having students work with one or two paragraphs at a time. Working with an entire paper at once can be a little overwhelming.) After quickly identifying their topics, students might create a T-graph of their topics and comments. This additional step sometimes makes it easier to see patterns. For example, we can take a sample paragraph from a student's paper on *All the Pretty Horses*.

> The code of the cowboy is one filled with honor, respect, and courage. The start of John Grady Cole's adventure sets off the violent scenes. He runs away with his best friend, Rawlins, and shortly after their departure they are joined by a younger, more stubborn and sensitive boy named Blevins. One night the companions ride into a lightning storm, which scares Blevins, and he ends up losing his horse and gun. They travel into the Mexican city of Encantada, and see Blevins' lost horse, which had been claimed by someone else. They attempt to steal the horse back and become separated while being chased by a posse pursuing them. In the act of bravery, violence is seen in their attempt to retrieve the horse. Violence here is displayed as part of the cowboy's honor. It displays the strength and the courage that the three young boys have.

We then can separate the paragraph's component sentences into topics and comments on a T-graph:

	Topic	Comment
1.	The code of the cowboy	is one filled with honor, respect, and courage.
2.	The start of John Grady Cole's adventure	sets off the violent scenes.
3.	He	runs away with his best friend, Rawlins, and shortly after their departure they are joined by a younger, more stubborn and sensitive boy named Blevins.
4.	One night the companions	ride into a lightning storm, which scares Blevins, and he ends up losing his horse and gun.
5.	They	travel into the Mexican city of Encantada, and see Blevins' lost horse, which had been claimed by someone else.
6.	They	attempt to steal the horse back and become separated while being chased by a posse pursuing them.
7.	In the act of bravery, violence	is seen in their attempt to retrieve the horse.
8.	Violence	here is displayed as part of the cowboy's honor.
9.	It	displays the strength and the courage that the three young boys have.

Students then can analyze their topical choices by answering some questions.

- How would you characterize the topics? As simple or complex?
- Are the topics concrete or abstract?
- Do the topics always function as sentence subjects?

In the preceding example, we see that while most of the topics are simple, the writer does begin with two topics that contain more complex nominal groups. The topics in sentences 1, 2, 7, and 8 are also abstract. However, there is also a series of sentences where the topics remain static—sentences 4–6—a sequence that might prompt some teachers to assess this part of the paragraph as too descriptive.

Tracing Known/New Information

In addition to having students analyze their topics, a teacher could also have students trace the known/new information in a paragraph from one of their drafts. In analyzing the development of information, we can find important junctures where the example paragraph breaks down. Immediately, we see the transition from the first sentence to the second in the previous example creates a problem. The first sentence establishes the paragraph as concerning "the code of the cowboy" and the role of "honor, respect, and courage" in that code. Yet, the second sentence introduces new information about violence without grammatically and logically connecting violence to the cowboy code or the code's attributes that are established in the prior sentence. The paragraph, then, continues for several sentences without providing any new information about the cowboy code until sentence 7, where bravery and violence are grammatically juxtaposed without elaboration. In fact, this moment serves a metaphor for the development of the paragraph as a whole: the student perceives a link between violence and the cowboy code, but that relationship is not made explicit. The closest the writer gets to articulating the link is in sentence 8. Still, even there, the linkage is rather ambiguous.

Looking at Conjunctive Resources

The disconnected nature of the information structure is also evident in the writer's use of conjunctive resources. As one would expect in a literary analysis paper, the writer uses resources of time: *after, one night, while*. The writer also repeatedly uses *and*—a resource of addition. The writer doesn't use, however, any resources of comparison (for example, *similarly, likewise, in contrast*) or any resources of consequence (for example, *because, therefore, nevertheless*). As a quick look at the conjunctive resources does here, having students identify and classify their conjunctive resources can reveal breaks in the logical development of students' argument.

Identifying and Classifying Verbs

Similar to identifying and classifying conjunctive resources, identifying and classifying verb process is yet another activity that can be made a part of students' revising. In the example paragraph, the student deploys primarily doing processes: *sets off, runs, are joined, ride, travel*, and so on. The writer also uses being processes: *is, become*. However, though there are a few sensing and thinking verbs (*see, is seen*), there are fewer than we might expect. The writer is concentrating far more on the actions of the characters than their internal, psychological world. Finally, the writer does not make any use of saying processes, which is also unusual. The writer is ignoring not just what the characters say, but also what the text says.

As students analyze verb process, they may also examine the participants in those processes. Do any of the processes have any unusual or unexpected participants? Are the participants physical or abstract? In our example, we see that the student, indeed, has included a mix of physical and abstract participants.

The inclusion of some abstract participants confirms an overall impression of the student's efforts at mimicking academic discourse, even if the student is not quite successful in this case.

Connecting Known and New Information

Chaining Information

There are a couple of final activities that teachers might consider in trying to integrate academic language awareness with the writing process. First, teachers might have students locate examples of chaining information in their essays. Chaining is a technique (using repetition, nominalization, or substitution) for picking up new information from a comment and making it known information in the following topic. It is a technique for connecting and developing information.

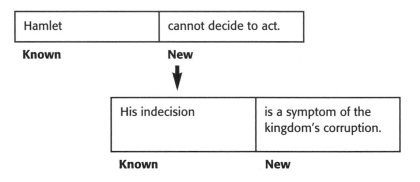

As I note in the book, chaining is not a technique that should be applied rigidly or mechanistically. However, we could reasonably ask students to use chaining three or four times in a five-paragraph essay. Thus, if a student is analyzing the information structure in a paragraph from an essay and chaining does not appear at all, a teacher could ask the student if there might be an appropriate place to use the technique. It may be that there isn't. However, if there are discontinuities in the information structure, as there are in our preceding example, the technique could help. In that paragraph, for example, chaining from the first sentence could help the student grammatically and logically connect the cowboy code to the theme of violence.

Clause Breakdowns

One last activity, which I mention in the book, is to have students break down parts of their essays not by sentences but by clauses. I know this might seem a daunting prospect. How reliably will my students be able to identify a clause? As much of a challenge as this may be, if students can recognize verbs, more often than not they can locate clauses. Also, the purpose of these activities isn't to have students unfailingly identify clauses. The purpose is to use clause breakdowns as tools to develop greater facility with language. Thus, it is more important for students to muck around and do their best than to have uniformly correct T-graphs.

The primary benefit of doing a clause versus a sentence breakdown is that the level of analysis of topic/comment and known/new can be more accurate and detailed. The sentence is a convenient unit because it is quick and easy for students to recognize, but the clause is the most basic unit where meaning gets made. There are other benefits, too, as recognizing clauses and their functions is essential for deliberate—as opposed to intuitive—punctuation.

A clause is conventionally defined as a grammatical unit that has a subject and a predicate. In other words, a clause has a subject and a verb. If students can locate verbs, then they can determine if the verb has a subject and is, therefore, part of a clause. I will provide an example of broken-down text in a moment, but first I would like to discuss a couple of complications.

The first is that, whenever possible, do not separate out adjectival clauses. These clauses begin with a relative pronoun (*that, which, who, whom*) or a relative adverb (*when, where*) and are often categorized as restrictive or nonrestrictive. As their name suggests, the function of these clauses is to modify a preceding noun or noun phrase. The following is an adjectival clause from the earlier example paragraph:

a lightning storm,	which scares Blevins,
Noun Phrase	**Adjectival Clause**

The adjectival clause modifies *storm*. It tells us which storm it is—the one that scares Blevins. Each of these also contains an adjectival clause.

- the shirt *that he wore*
- the restaurant *where we ate*
- the student *who aced the test*
- the era *when pitchers ruled baseball*

The clause together with the noun (or noun phrase) it modifies can be replaced with a pronoun (*he, she, it, they,* and so on). We don't break these out into separate clauses on our T-graphs because these clauses are functioning as adjectives. With the noun that they modify, they form a nominal group, which is why a personal pronoun can be substituted for the group as a whole. The sentence in which the "storm" example appears, therefore, would be separated as follows.

1.	One night the companions	ride into a lightning storm, which scares Blevins,
2.	and he	ends up losing his horse and gun.

Adjectival clauses can sometimes present problems because the words that serve as cues (*that, which, who, whom, when, where*) have many other functions. For example, *that* can appear after verbs of saying and verbs of sensing and thinking. In a paragraph that we will be looking at shortly, a student writes, "Hamlet reasons that murdering Claudius in prayer would be 'hire and salary, not revenge' (III.iii.84)." In this case, *that* is not signaling an adjectival clause, it is signaling a projected clause. We might think of these clauses as the speech and thought bubbles that appear in cartoons: *says that . . . , wonders that . . . , feels that . . . , states that . . .* , and so on.

These clauses come after verbs (rather than nouns) and they function as clauses (rather than adjectives), so we would break them apart.

1.	Hamlet	reasons
2.	that murdering Claudius in prayer	would be "hire and salary, not revenge" (III.iii.84).

One last complication can arise with coordinated clauses (clauses joined by *and, but, or, so, for, nor,* or *yet*). In these constructions, we can have multiple verbs with the subject appearing only once. The student analyzing *Hamlet*, for example, writes, "Claudius did not actually confess and would have gone straight to hell." Here, *Claudius* is the subject of two coordinated verbs—*did (not) confess* and *would have gone*—but the second instance is implied rather than stated explicitly. These clauses should be separated:

1.	Claudius	did not actually confess
2.	and [Claudius]	would have gone straight to hell.

As I said, I know this can seem daunting, but, again, the purpose is to get students working with language, not having students generate perfect T-graphs. To see how clause-level analysis can work, let's look at a sample text. Below is part of a paragraph from a student's essay on *Hamlet*.

> When Hamlet finds Claudius defenseless and kneeling in prayer, he quickly draws his sword. However, his moment of audacity is cut short by his cowardice and reflection. Once again, Hamlet's unnecessary observation keeps him from taking the life of Claudius. Hamlet reasons that murdering Claudius in prayer would be "hire and salary, not revenge" (III.iii.84). When Hamlet departs, the reader learns that Claudius did not actually confess and would have gone straight to hell if Hamlet had killed him instead of thinking about the consequences of his actions. Hamlet's plans continually "turn awry and lose the name of action" (III.i.95–96), which leads to his demise. He only succeeds in killing Claudius after he has been poisoned by Laertes' rapier and his own death is imminent. In a sense, Hamlet only takes action when he has no time left to think. His indecisiveness markedly brings him to ruin.

Here is a sentence-level T-graph of the paragraph.

	Topic	Comment
1.	When Hamlet finds Claudius defenseless and kneeling in prayer,	he quickly draws his sword.
2.	However, his moment of audacity	is cut short by his cowardice and reflection.
3.	Once again, Hamlet's unnecessary observation	keeps him from taking the life of Claudius.
4.	Hamlet	reasons that murdering Claudius in prayer would be "hire and salary, not revenge" (III.iii.84).
5.	When Hamlet	departs, the reader learns that Claudius did not actually confess and would have gone straight to hell if Hamlet had killed him instead of thinking about the consequences of his actions.
6.	Hamlet's plans	continually "turn awry and lose the name of action" (III.i.95–96), which leads to his demise.
7.	He	only succeeds in killing Claudius after he has been poisoned by Laertes' rapier and his own death is imminent.
8.	In a sense, Hamlet	only takes action when he has no time left to think.
9.	His indecisiveness	markedly brings him to ruin.

Based on the T-graph, what kinds of evaluations would you make about the topics, comments, and information structure?

Here, now, is clause-level T-graph.

	Topic	Comment
1.	When Hamlet	finds Claudius defenseless and kneeling in prayer,
2.	he	quickly draws his sword.
3.	However, his moment of audacity	is cut short by his cowardice and reflection.
4.	Once again, Hamlet's unnecessary observation	keeps him from taking the life of Claudius.
5.	Hamlet	reasons

	Topic	Comment
6.	that murdering Claudius in prayer	would be "hire and salary, not revenge" (III.iii.84).
7.	When Hamlet	departs,
8.	the reader	learns
9.	that Claudius	did not actually confess
10.	and [Claudius]	would have gone straight to hell
11.	if Hamlet	had killed him instead of thinking about the consequences of his actions.
12.	Hamlet's plans	continually "turn awry and lose the name of action" (III.i.95–96), which leads to his demise.
13.	He	only succeeds in killing Claudius
14.	after he	has been poisoned by Laertes' rapier
15.	and his own death	is imminent.
16.	In a sense, Hamlet	only takes action
17.	when he	has no time left to think.
18.	His indecisiveness	markedly brings him to ruin.

How does this added detail affect the kinds of evaluations you would make?

AUTHORING ASSESSMENTS

I did not include any assessments in the book because I wanted the lessons to be as flexible as possible. I didn't want to tie teachers to a prescribed timetable or to standardized evaluations. My decision not to make assessments part of the book should not, however, be taken to mean that assessing students on the content of the lessons is inappropriate. The code-switching lessons in particular contain a great deal of declarative knowledge for which students might reasonably be held accountable.

Fortunately, assessing students need not be complicated or time consuming. In fact, unlike a lot of English classroom content, the content of the code-switching lessons lends itself rather easily to multiple-choice and fill-in-the-blank quizzes. Teachers can model assessments on the activities in the lessons themselves.

Such assessments, of course, require sentences or bits of text that have the grammatical features under study. If a teacher is going to ask students, "Which of the following sentences uses habitual *be*?" or direct them, "Code-switch the underlined Vernacular features in the following paragraph," that teacher is faced with two options: either find existing examples, as I do in the book, or make them up.

My first piece of advice would be this: *Do not make up an example of a feature that you yourself do not use.*

People who are not speakers of a particular variety of English often make grammatical mistakes when they try to imitate that variety. In trying to parody the use of habitual *be*, for example, a *Washington Post* columnist writes the following:

> "What you be talkin' 'bout, my man?" he said. "I don't be offerin' you my grub; I be sayin' hello. You know, like, what's up?" (Raspberry 1996)

He doesn't even get it right once in this passage. The first instance ("What you be talkin' 'bout") should be a zero copula ("What you talkin' 'bout"). The second ("I don't be offerin' you") is a present tense negative, so it should use *ain't* ("I ain't offerin' you"). The third ("I be sayin' hello") is in the first person, so the copular verb needs to be present ("I'm sayin' hello").

This kind of parody brings me to my second piece of advice: *If you use the Internet to find examples of a feature, make sure that the examples use the feature correctly.*

The Internet is a great resource. Song lyrics, for example, are abundant online and can be engaging illustrations. Just be sure that any examples you choose are accurate representations of the feature on which you want to quiz students. As the *Washington Post* excerpt suggests, people sometimes parody features, particularly shibboleths, and those parodies can be wildly erroneous.

My third and final piece of advice would be: *Don't confuse written representations of sound with grammar and syntax.*

In the *Washington Post* excerpt, we can find some written representations of sound. The writer, for example, denotes the pronunciation of the *-ing* ending as *-in'*. This, of course, is a common convention and because of that convention, many people refer to the latter pronunciation as "*g*-dropping." The reality, however, is that the *g* isn't dropped at all because it isn't pronounced either way. No one says the *g-* sound in *goal* at the end of *-ing*. The first pronunciation represented by the standard spelling is made with the back of the tongue pressing on the soft part of the back of the palate, and the sound is made through the nose. (Just try to make the sound while plugging your nose.) The second pronunciation represented by leaving off the *g* is made with the tip of the tongue pressing on the upper ridge behind the teeth, and the sound is also made through the nose. No sound is being "dropped." Rather, the place of articulation is moving from the back of the palate to the front.

Now, teachers aren't likely to ask students to code-switch *talkin'* to *talking*. However, I have seen teachers ask students to code-switch *dat* to *that*. As with the *talking/talkin'* distinction, *that* and *dat* can be described by differences in where consonants are pronounced. The *th-* sound in *that* is made with the tongue behind the upper front teeth and the *d-* sound in *dat* is made with the tip of the tongue pressing on the upper ridge behind the teeth, and both sounds are made with the vocal chords active. (You can put a finger on your neck below your chin and feel your vocal chords vibrate when you make each sound.) Additionally, the *th-* sound is made by forcing air around the tongue and through the teeth, and the *d-* sound is made by stopping the flow of air.

These differences in pronunciation, like differences in grammar and syntax, can be described and are systematic. Pronunciation and grammar are, however, distinct processes and should not be confused. In the cases of *talking/talkin'* and *that/dat*, we are describing differences in what linguists call *phonology*. Though the words in each pair may be pronounced differently, they have the same grammatical function and mean the same thing.

Phonology and phonological variation are interesting subjects of study, but I do not cover them in *In Other Words*. If teachers wish to explore phonology, they certainly can. It is important, however, not to ask students to perform phonological code-switching under the rubric of grammar.

All of these suggestions should provide you with some additional help and support. I may be a geek for saying so, but language and grammar can be fascinating. My greatest hope is that the book serves to put English grammar in a new light and inspires classrooms to develop their own investigations into the workings of language.

notes

1   If you would like more information about English phonology or more detailed information about English grammar, refer to the work of Curzan and Adams (2006) listed in the bibliography.

2   The idea for a core graphic organizer was suggested by Rebecca Wheeler in a personal communication (2008). For more ideas on how to create and use contrastive exercises, please refer to Wheeler's own work (2005) and the work she has coauthored with Rachel Swords (2004, 2006), which are listed in the bibliography.

3   The notations "V + -ed" and "V + -ed/en" come from Morenberg (1991). For more information on this topic, refer to his work listed in the bibliography.

4   For more information about code-switching, see the work of Wheeler (2005), Wheeler and Swords (2004, 2006), Rickford (2000), and Rickford and Rickford (2000) in the bibliography.

5   The quotation is taken from Coopman, Hart, Hougland, and Billings (1998).

6   If you would like more information about language variety in the United States, see the work of Reaser and Wolfram (2008) and Wolfram, Adger, and Christian (1999); if you would like a more in-depth look at African American English, see Green (2002) in the bibliography.

7   To find out more about topics and comments (themes and rhemes) in particular, or academic language in general, see Schleppegrell (2004).

8   The term "known/new contract" comes from Kolln (1991). Refer to her work in the bibliography for other information about known/new and rhetorically related grammar.

9   The division of conjunctive resources into these categories comes from Martin and Rose (2007). For more information on conjunctive resources, refer to their work listed in the bibliography.

10   See Schleppegrell (2004) for more information about process types.

11   Staples, Brent. 1997. "The Last Train from Oakland." *New York Times*, A30.

12   This prompt is adapted from an assignment authored by Anne Curzan.

13   Nunberg, Geoffrey. 2001. *The Way We Talk Now: Commentaries on Language and Culture from NPR's "Fresh Air."* Boston: Houghton Mifflin.

glossary

accent The systematic pronunciation of a dialect.

adjective By function, an adjective modifies a noun. By form, an adjective can have comparative and superlative forms, either by adding the suffixes *-er* and *-est* or the adverbs *more* and *most*.

aspect Indicates the perception of an action by a speaker (like whether that action is complete or habitual). What is commonly called the *progressive tense*, therefore, is really a progressive aspect.

auxiliary verb A verb that works in combination with a main verb. Together an auxiliary verb (or verbs) with the main verb form a verb phrase.

code-switch To alternate or change from one grammatically distinct language variety to another. In second language teaching, the term can be applied to a speaker who switches between languages like Spanish and English. Here the term applies to any speaker (or writer) who switches between varieties of English with contrasting grammatical systems (usually a Vernacular variety and a Standard one, though that does not have to be the case).

comment The part of the sentence or clause that follows the topic. It is the place where the writer develops the message of the sentence or clause, where the writer "comments on" the topic.

conjunction The most common conjunctions are coordinating conjunctions, which connect words to words, phases to phrases, or clauses to clauses. Some frequently used examples are *and*, *but*, *or,* and *so*. The second most common conjunctions are subordinating conjunctions, which connect a dependent clause to a main clause. Some frequently used examples are *because*, *when*, *after,* and *if*.

conjunctive resources Words or phrases (including coordinating conjunctions, subordinating conjunctions, and conjunctive adverbs) used to logically connect sentences or parts of sentences. Four basic categories of logical relation include addition, comparison, time, and consequence.

descriptive grammar Rules of language that describe how people communicate. Descriptive grammar, which seeks to explain the systematic nature of all language, is distinct from prescriptive grammar, which advocates for certain usage conventions.

dialect A variety of a language that is systematically distinct from other varieties.

discourse marker A word or phrase that divides or organizes spoken discourse into units.

genre A group of texts with common rhetorical and grammatical characteristics.

grammar The organization and structure of language that enable people to communicate with each other.

infinitive The unmarked form of a verb. That is, there is no indication of person, number, or time. Often, the infinitive is expressed with the particle *to*.

known/new contract The preference for information that is known to come before information that is new in a sentence or clause.

nominalization Converting a word that isn't a noun, like a verb or adjective, into a noun.

noun By function, a noun is a word that can be the subject or object of a verb. By form, most nouns can be preceded by an article (*a/an/the*). Also, in Standard

English, most regular nouns can accept the plural marker -s and the possessive marker -'s.

perfect aspect An aspect indicating the relationship between a previous state or action and one occurring at a later time or describing a previous state or action from the point of view of a later time. In Standard English, the perfect aspect can be expressed in the past, present, and future, as well as progressively and conditionally. In the past, present, and future, the perfect aspect combines the appropriate form of *have* with a main verb (V + -ed/en, or what's commonly called the past participle).

predicative adjective An adjective joined to the noun that it modifies by a linking verb (as opposed to an attributive adjective, which usually precedes the noun that it modifies).

preposition A word that expresses the relationship of a noun or noun equivalent to another noun, adjective, or verb, typically relationships of location, duration, direction, and manner. Some common prepositions are *of*, *in*, *to*, *for*, *on*, *with*, *at*, *by*, and *from*.

progressive aspect An aspect indicating an ongoing or continuing action. In Standard English, the progressive combines a form of *be* with a main verb (V + -ing, or what's commonly called the *present participle*).

register A collection of linguistic features customarily used for a particular rhetorical practice.

tense A change in the form of a verb indicating whether an action or state takes place in past or nonpast time. Strictly speaking, Standard English has only two tenses: the present and the past. In the present and the past, the verb changes form—it is marked with an ending or changes pronunciation/spelling—to indicate whether it is past or nonpast: *wails* versus *wailed* or *write* versus *wrote*. In order to express other information about actions or events, English varieties make extensive use of auxiliary verbs as part of systems of aspect and mood.

topic The beginning of a sentence or clause. Because of its initial position, it is both grammatically and thematically important.

verb By function, a verb is a word that can accept a subject. By form, verbs can be marked for time (like past time, for example, by adding -ed to regular verbs in Standard English). Also, in Standard English, most verbs can accept the third-person singular marker -s in present (nonpast) time and can accept -ing to form the progressive.

vernacular A variety of English that has systematic grammatical differences from Standard English.

zero copula A grammatical construction in which the linking (or so-called *copular*) verb between the subject and predicate is implied, rather than explicitly stated. In some Vernacular varieties of English, the zero copula can be used with predicative adjectives: "she just tired" (*A Raisin in the Sun*). They can also be used with predicative nouns: "You a horrible-looking chick at this hour" (*A Raisin in the Sun*). Note that in these Vernaculars, the linking verb can be absent only in the present tense (*is*, *are*) and that the linking verb (*am*) must be there in the first-person singular.

"ain't." 1983. *Webster's Ninth New Collegiate Dictionary*. Springfield, MA: Merriam-Webster.

"ain't." 2000. *The American Heritage Dictionary of the English Language*. 4th ed. Boston: Houghton Mifflin.

"ain't." 2006. Urban Dictionary. Available from www.urbandictionary.com.

Angelou, Maya. 1997. *I Know Why the Caged Bird Sings*. New York: Bantam Books.

Associated Press. 2005. Hilton: "I'm Like an American Princess." MSNBC, May 4. Available from www.msnbc.msn.com.

———. 2007a. Bonds Moves into Eternity, Assumes MLB Home Run Record. ESPN, August 8. Available from http://espn.go.com.

———. 2007b. Thunderstorms Batter Ohio, Pa., Killing 1. *USA Today*, August 10. Available from www.usatoday.com.

Austen, Jane. 2008. *Pride and Prejudice*. Project Guttenberg. Available from www.gutenberg.org.

Bailey, Richard W. 1995. Reviews—the Story of Webster's Third: Philip Gove's Controversial Dictionary and Its Critics by Herbert C. Morton. *Language* 71(3):604.

Baugh, John. 2000. *Beyond Ebonics: Linguistic Pride and Racial Prejudice*. New York: Oxford University Press.

BBC News. 2004. Google "Saved" Australian Hostage. BBC News, October 19. Available from http://news.bbc.co.uk.

Bring It On. 2000. Universal City: Universal Pictures.

Brontë, Charlotte. 2008. *Jane Eyre*. Project Guttenberg. Available from www.gutenberg.org.

Buckley, Norman. 2005. The Pot Stirrer. In *The OC*. USA: Warner Brothers Television.

Bush, George W. 2005. President Holds Press Conference, edited by Office of the Press Secretary. Available from www.whitehouse.gov.

Calloway, Sway. 2004. Jay-Z: 99 Problems, Hundreds of Rumors. MTV, April 28. Available from www.mtv.com.

Carter, Kelley L. 2007. TI Connects with His Fans. *Detroit Free Press*, August 12. Available from www.freep.com.

Carter, Thomas. 2001. Save the Last Dance. USA: Paramount Pictures.

Casablanca, Ted. 2006. The Awful Truth. E! Online, October 17. Available from www.eonline.com.

Chaucer, Geoffrey. 2008. *The Canterbury Tales*. Project Guttenberg. Available from www.gutenberg.org.

Christie, Frances. 2005. *Language Education in the Primary Years*. Sydney, Australia: UNSW Press.

Chu, Jeff. 2005. Who Wants to Be an Iraqi Star? *Time,* August 28. Available from www.time.com.

Clueless. 1995. USA: Paramount Pictures.

Concrete. 2005. Don Cannon. *Concrete.* Available from www.concretemag.com.

Coopman, Stephanie J., Joy Hart, James G. Hougland Jr., and Dwight B. Billings.

1998. Speaking for God: The Functions of Church Leader Storytelling in Southern Appalachia in the 1950s. *American Communication Journal* 1(2). Available from www.acjounral.org.

Coultas, Jimmy. 2006. DJ Premier. *Plastic Soup.* Available from www.plasticsoup.com.

Crawford, Byron. 2007. The New Biggie Album. *XXL Magazine*, February 28. Available from www.xxlmag.com.

Crosley, Hillary. 2007. 50 Cent Still Confident in Sales Battle with Kanye. *Billboard,* September 14. Available from www.billboard.com.

Curzan, Anne, and Michael Adams. 2006. *How English Works: A Linguistic Introduction.* New York: Pearson/Longman.

DiLeo, Adam. 2007. The Crow: Stairway to Heaven Review. *IGN,* July 31. Available from http://dvd.ign.com.

"dog." 2008. Merriam-Webster Online Dictionary. Available from www.merriam-webster.com.

Donovan, Tate. 2005. The Game. In *The OC*. USA: Warner Brothers Television.

Douglas, Laura. 2008. CMT Insider Interview: Alan Jackson. *CMT,* February 29. Available from www.cmt.com.

Duncan-Mao, Andréa. 2006. Lil' Kim: It Has Been Said. *XXL Magazine*, March 24. Available from www.xxlmag.com.

Epstein, Daniel Robert. 2004. Jay-Z Interview. *Underground Online.* Available from www.ugo.com.

Feinsand, Mark. 2007. Yankees Facing Rival, Survival. *New York Daily News*, June 1. Available from www.nydailynews.com.

Finding Nemo. 2003. USA: Buena Vista Pictures.

Fine, Jason. 2000. Cash Money's Midnight Ride. Review of Reviewed Item. *Rolling Stone* (840). Available from www.rollingstone.com.

Frontline. 1999. Smoke in the Eye: Interview with Walter Cronkite. Available from www.pbs.org/wgbh/pages/frontline.

Graves, Jen. 2006. Slog News and Arts. *The Stranger Weekly*, August 6. Available from http://slog.thestranger.com.

Green, Lisa J. 2002. *African American English: A Linguistic Introduction*. Cambridge: Cambridge University Press.

Hakim, Danny. 2004. Fo Shizzle, That Big Bad Chrysler Really Does Sizzle. *New York Times*, C1.

Hall, Fitzedward. 1873. *Modern English*. New York: Scribner Armstrong & Co.

Hammond, Candy. 2008. Pop Goes the Culture: Disney's Dresses and Kitty Cafes. *Cape Cod Times*, April 7. Available from www.capecodonline.com.

Hansberry, Lorraine. 1995. *A Raisin in the Sun*. New York: The Modern Library.

Herman, Lewis Helmar, and Marguerite Shalett Herman. 1947. *American Dialects: A Manual for Actors, Directors, and Writers*. New York: Theatre Art Books.

Higgins, Matt. 2007. Surf's Up, and Upscale, as Sport Reverses Its Beach Bum Image. *New York Times*, February 11, 11.

Hurston, Zora Neale. 2006. *Their Eyes Were Watching God*. New York: Harper Perennial Modern Classics.

Johnson, Samuel. 1752. *The Rambler*. 6 vols. Vol. 6. London: printed for J. Payne.

Kamen, Al. 2006. Diplomacy Ain't What It Used to Be. *The Washington Post*, A21.

King, Dr. Martin Luther, Jr. 1963. *Letter from a Birmingham Jail*. The King Center, cited April 6, 2008. Available from www.thekingcenter.org.

King, Larry. 2001. A Look Back at President George Bush in His Own Words. CNN, January 27. Available from http://transcripts.cnn.com.

Kolln, Martha. 1991. *Rhetorical Grammar: Grammatical Choices, Rhetorical Effects*. New York: Macmillan.

Lee, Harper. 2006. *To Kill a Mockingbird*. New York: Harper Perennial.

Levy, Collin. 2007. Mack the Nice. *The Wall Street Journal*, August 2. Available from http://online.wsj.com.

Lippi-Green, Rosina. 1997. *English with an Accent: Language, Ideology, and Discrimination in the United States*. New York: Routledge.

Mannix, Chris. 2008. Rocket Boosters: Supporting Cast Key for Houston During Stretch Run. *Sports Illustrated*, March 5. Available from http://sportsillustrated.cnn.com.

Martin, J. R., and David Rose. 2007. *Working with Discourse: Meaning Beyond the Clause*. 2nd ed. London: Continuum.

McCarthy, Cormac. 1992. *All the Pretty Horses*. New York: Knopf

McCarthy, Todd. 2006. Movie Review: The Da Vinci Code. *Variety,* May 16. Available from www.variety.com.

Mean Girls. 2004. USA: Paramount Pictures.

Morenberg, Max. 1991. *Doing Grammar*. New York: Oxford University Press.

Morrison, Toni. 2000. *The Bluest Eye*. New York: Knopf.

Mossé, Fernand. 1968. *A Handbook of Middle English*. 5th print., corr. and augm. ed. Baltimore, MD: Johns Hopkins Press.

NASCAR. 2008. Press Release: NASCAR Teleconference—Dale Earnhardt Jr., Sam Hornish Jr., & Denny Hamlin. January 28. Available from www.motorsport.com.

Norris, Patrick. 2003. The Heights. In *The OC*. USA: Warner Brothers Television.

Pickrell, Emily. 2007. iPhone Sales "Staggering" Yet Lower Than Expected. *Newsday*, August 25. Available from www.newsday.com.

Pirates of the Caribbean: The Curse of the Black Pearl. 2003. USA: Buena Vista Pictures.

Raspberry, William. 1996. "To Throw in a Lot of 'Bes,' or Not? A Conversation on Ebonics." *Washington Post*, A27.

Reaser, Jeffery, and Walt Wolfram. 2008. *Voices of North Carolina Dialect Awareness Curriculum*. North Carolina State University Linguistics Program. Available from www.ncsu.edu/linguistics/research_ dialecteducation.php.

Rickford, John R. 2000. Using the Vernacular to Teach the Standard. In *Ebonics in the Urban Education Debate, Revised*, edited by J. D. Ramirez, T. G. Wiley, G. de Klerk and E. Lee. Long Beach, CA: Center for Language Minority Education and Research. 23-41.

Rickford, John R., and Russell John Rickford. 2000. *Spoken Soul: The Story of Black English*. New York: Wiley.

Salters, Lisa. 2001. "World News Now," first broadcast on September 12 by ABC News.

Schleppegrell, Mary. 2004. *The Language of Schooling: A Functional Linguistics Perspective*. Mahwah, NJ: Lawrence Erlbaum Associates.

Scott, A. O. 2006. "Talladega Nights": The Men Are Rowdy, the Cars Are Fast and the Product Placement Is Extreme. *The New York Times*, August 4, E13.

Shakespeare, William. 2008a. *As You Like It*. Project Guttenberg. Available from www.gutenberg.org.

——. 2008b. *The Tragedy of Hamlet, Prince of Denmark*. Project Guttenberg. Available from www.gutenberg.org.

Shaw, Bernard. 1916. *Androcles and the Lion; Overruled; Pygmalion*. New York: Brentano's.

Shpigel, Ben. 2006. For Mets, Two Out of Three Ain't Bad. *New York Times*, May 26, D1.

Siebert, T.W. 1998. Chris Tucker: The Well Rounded Interview. Well Rounded Entertainment, September. Available from www.well-rounded.com.

Smith, Steven. 1997. Cooler Than Mr. Freeze. *Los Angeles Times*, June 19, F6.

Smitherman, Geneva. 1977. *Talkin and Testifyin: The Language of Black America*. Boston: Houghton Mifflin.

——. 2000. *Talkin That Talk: Language, Culture, and Education in African America*. London: Routledge.

Society for Pure English. 1919. *S.P.E. Tract*. Vol. 1. Oxford: Clarendon Press.

Steinbeck, John. 1993. *Of Mice and Men*. New York: Penguin Books.

——. 1996. *The Grapes of Wrath and Other Writings, 1936–1941*. New York: Literary Classics of the United States.

"surfing." 2007. Microsoft® Encarta® Online Encyclopedia. Available from http://encarta.msn.com.

Taylor, Claire. 2004. SJSU "American Idol" Contestant Hopes to Overcome TV Pressure. *Spartan Daily*, March 9. Available from www.thespartandaily.com/.

Terrell, Mary Church. 1906. *What It Means to Be Colored in Capital of the U.S.* Historical Documents in United States History. Available from www.historicaldocuments.com.

The Little Mermaid. 1989. USA: Buena Vista Pictures.

Toynton, Ian. 2005. The Mallpisode. In *The OC*. USA: Warner Brothers Television.

Twain, Mark. 2008. *The Adventures of Huckleberry Finn*. Project Guttenberg. Available from www.gutenberg.org.

Valley Girl. 1983. USA: MGM Home Entertainment.

Voepel, Mechelle. 2006. Monarchs Know They Let Title Slip Away. ESPN, September 10. Available from http://espn.go.com.

Walker, Alice. 1992. *The Color Purple*. New York: Harcourt Brace Jovanovich.

WH. 2002. Movie Review: Brown Sugar. *Time Out/London*. Available from www.timeout.com.

Wharmby, Tony. 2005. The Rager. In *The OC*. USA: Warner Brothers Television.

Wheeler, Rebecca S. 2005. Code-Switch to Teach Standard English. *English Journal* 94(5):108–112.

Wheeler, Rebecca S., and Rachel Swords. 2004. Codeswitching: Tools of Language and Culture Transform the Dialectally Diverse Classroom. *Language Arts* 81(6):470–480.

——. 2006. *Code-Switching: Teaching Standard English in Urban Classrooms, Theory & Research into Practice*. Urbana, IL: National Council of Teachers of English.

Whitlock, Jason. 2006. An Honest Look at NFL QBs. ESPN. Available from http://espn.go.com.

Williams, Carnet. 2007. *Bagus Surf*, February 6. Available from http://surfbagus.org.

Wilson, August. 1990. *The Piano Lesson*. New York: Plume.

——. 2003. *Fences*. Alexandria, VA: Alexander Street Press.

Wolfram, Walt, Carolyn Temple Adger, and Donna Christian. 1999. *Dialects in Schools and Communities*. Mahwah, NJ: Lawrence Erlbaum Associates.

WOWT. 2008. Freshman Female Wrestler Turning Heads, Pinning Opponents. WOWT, January 11. Available from www.wowt.com.

X, Malcolm. 1964. Ballot or Bullet. CMG Worldwide. Available from http://blackhistory.cmgworldwide.com.